Becoming

Wonderfully

Balanced

A Memoir and Guidebook to Living a Healthy Lifestyle Led by God

I dedicate this book to the only people who made this book happen- my awesome parents. My mother, Jennifer Kraus and my father, Thomas Kraus, the best support system I can think of. I am eternally grateful for the endless support, love, and Godly encouragement you gave me throughout the tough years and the happy years.

Contents

Note from the Author:

Past experience. What a topic. Not many people want to think about their past, let alone write about their past experiences, especially when they are full of struggles, bad choices, and difficult circumstances. This is why I'm here to tell you mine. I'm here to be real. I'm here to be vulnerable. I'm here to share what my past lifestyle looked like for me and how I'm beginning to grow and learn from it. Are you ready?

Digging Deep ....Chapter 1

"I praise you because I am fearfully and wonderfully made;
your works are wonderful, I know that full well."

Psalm 139:14

Let's go back to the early years, about one year ago and beyond. Growing up I always (and I mean always) ate whatever I wanted. My parents were not those type of parents who restricted their children from having sugar, nor did they really even restrict us from eating what we wanted. In fact, the rule was as long as we ate our dinner, we were allowed dessert. Dessert was pretty much a staple in our house-I'm talking ice cream and brownie desserts. So, as you can imagine, I ate what I wanted and I gave no cares to it because in the end, what was stopping me? Nothing.

You're probably wondering, "Were you overweight?" and the answer is no. Not at all. In fact, I was always looked at as the "super tiny" and "petite" one of my age group. At my yearly checkups, I was placed in the lower percentile of weight and height. I was shorter and thinner than all of my friends. My Mom always said I had not one ounce of fat on me. This wasn't abnormal either. Every one of my family members had a tiny figure. We were all pretty active, growing up playing sports like upwards basketball and soccer. I was constantly moving. Naturally, my metabolism was working overtime (literally killing off all of the calories I was eating).

Going into middle school was when this "petite" image started to bother me. I was done with being smaller than all of my friends. They fit into American Eagle jeans and I had to shop at Target and Old Navy. Tragic, am I right? At least this was the most "tragic" thing I had to worry about. I didn't want to be called a "twig" anymore. I hated this title. I was always a little insecure about my body image, figure, and clothing sizes. I just wanted to fit into the fashion that fit the culture of my school.

I stayed this short, petite, and undeveloped size until high school. It was the first month of freshman year that I started my menstrual cycle for the first time. Most girls dread this occurrence, but it gave me some relief. I thought, "Now I'm finally like all of the other girls." This was it. Now I would start to grow and maybe, just maybe, even get boobs! (Yes I actually thought all of these things. The world feeds a lot into your mind, believe it or not).

Turns out, I was right, about the growing that is. By the end of freshman year, I had grown about three inches. Incredible. I was at the height or taller than most of my friends, but I was still skinny. In fact, I stayed skinny. I continued to eat what I wanted throughout all of high school. Summers were spent with friends consuming all of the half-off Sonic slushies, ice cream, and Cookout milkshakes I desired. I pretty much ate like a typical American child and I saw nothing wrong with that. Then the colder months came, which meant tons and tons of baked goods. Baked goods which, yes, I made all by myself (important: baking is my thing, always has been). I baked all sorts of things: pies, cakes, bread, and alllll types of cookies-gingerbread and pumpkin cookies... can I get an AMEN?

I continued with this way of eating for a while and it never really bothered me, nor did I ever pay attention to it. I also continued to stay active. My freshman and sophomore year of high school, and during the summer in between those years, I played lacrosse. I went to conditioning during the fall and winter, which consisted of tons of running, and played the sport throughout the spring and summer. As you can tell, I was pretty active, so eating the way I did really had no physical effect on me, at least from the outside.

It wasn't until the end of my sophomore year that I started to take notice of what I was eating. PAUSE. I should probably explain to you my schooling situation during this time.

Freshman year I attended Woodmont High School. Beginning sophomore year, I also attended Woodmont, for about a month that is. In the end of September, I received a phone call from Brashier Middle College Charter High School (what a mouthful) informing me that I had been offered a spot into their school. I said yes right away. I don't know what it was in me that made me say yes, but I said yes and went for it. I did not sleep on it. I did not think on it. I just said yes.

After a month of attending this strangely small school (about ¼ of the size of Woodmont), I began to make friends. By the end of sophomore year, these friends had become best friends. I spent every waking moment with these girls. Now, you're caught up. Which means… UNPAUSE.

April 2015… Young Kids on a Diet uh-oh

My new friends at this new school were (still are) the most petite human beings ever. We were all pretty petite, but I didn't always feel so petite around them. Apparently they didn't feel too petite either because towards the end of sophomore year, my two friends and I had come up with a plan to go on a paleo diet. Why? I have no clue. We all had the common thought running across our minds that bread and carbs and basically anything that tasted good, was bad for our bodies. Our goal was to complete a whole month of this diet with a "cheat" day once a week. Our overall goal was to lose weight we thought we so desperately needed to lose. And this was when the comparison game was first planted in my brain. I believe this was one of the turning points that would set the stage for my struggles in the not so distant future.

This fad diet did not last very long for me, but the feelings I had developed about certain foods would be rooted deep within me and have a greater impact in the future. No longer did I eat whatever I wanted and have no cares about it. For the most part, I ate whatever I wanted, but now, I started to have feelings of guilt about it.

August 2015... Processed Lies

Junior year was when these feelings turned from being just feelings to actions. Junior year was the year my eating habits and lifestyle took a complete 180. Everything that I thought I knew about health was being instilled into my brain and therefore, into my eating habits.
Since I know you're wondering, what I thought I knew was that all carbs are bad for me. Bread is bad for me, sugar is bad for me, all candy is bad for me, processed food is bad for me, and dairy is bad for me. Although a few of those statements have a little bit of truth in them, once you dig a little deeper into their context, falsehood can be found in each of those statements which is what will be explained later on. Stay tuned folks.

Along with information I was pouring into my brain from numerous articles and Pinterest boards, a few other factors affected my change in eating. In fact, this is where my friends, who I explained earlier, come into play. I began to look at these girls in my life and think, "They are so tiny. Why am I not tiny? I need to lose weight." The way I viewed myself was slowly starting to be affected by the way I viewed these girls and how their physical stature was designed. I didn't like the way I was designed.

Another factor that played into my eating habits was the medical status of my gallbladder. Around the months of July and August I started experiencing pain in my stomach.

Whether I ate or did not eat, I was experiencing these pains. After a few weeks of undergoing this pain, Mamma thought it was smart to pay a visit to the doctor, so we did exactly that. After many tests, an ultrasound, and an MRI, the doctor discovered that it was the effects of my gallbladder failing. No longer was my gallbladder doing the job that it needed to do, to filter and digest the fatty foods that I was eating.

Because of the results of my gallbladder, I assumed two things: 1) it was because of my horrible junk-food eating that my gallbladder was failing and 2) I needed to eat healthier to stop the excruciating pain I was having. From then on, I was going to stop the endless amounts of milkshakes, ice cream, cookies, and any other junk food you can think of. Not yet, had this become obsessive whatsoever. At this point I was only cutting the junk food out of my life, a step that was good for me, and would be good for anybody.

December... Baby it's Cold Outside

After receiving the results, my mother and I scheduled an appointment to get my gallbladder removed. December fifth was when this surgery was to occur. December finally arrived and it was time for my surgery to take place. As I have been with any medical issue/event in the past, I was calm and ready (two descriptive words you would not expect many 16-year old's to feel under these circumstances). The surgery went great. Everything went just as planned. As proof I have 4 beautiful scars on my stomach. Forever. How wonderful. (Can you sense the sarcasm?)

Now, the next step, recovery. What a fun process this was... I could not eat anything normal for at least a week. Without a gallbladder, my digestive system now had no way of digesting fatty foods. Meaning, my body had to adjust to this new way of digesting food. For a week I ate nothing but super bland soups, applesauce, and crackers. Under these dietary restrictions, I began to lose weight, which was expected. The amount of weight I was losing was not a danger to my body at all. What was a danger was the way I reacted to this weight loss and the way I reacted to other circumstances; also during this time, my friend was experiencing the same thing-surgery affecting weight loss that is. Not only was she experiencing weight loss but more weight loss than me. Being that I am a teenage girl, as you may be, I have a slightly competitive mindset and of course, a few insecurities. Which means these circumstances did not rest easy with me. Slowly I started to develop a sense of jealousy. A little ridiculous right? I was jealous that I wasn't losing a significant amount of weight. Hmmm. This jealousy then created insecurities. Slowly, I was developing insecurities about my body that I never thought I would have. Most of the insecurities I had towards myself revolved around the scale. I started looking at the scale, something I never did or even cared about before.

Bye Bye Peanut Butter Fudge Milkshakes

My sole purpose in eating healthy was to 1) cut out all junk food because it'll make me gain weight, 2) drop the number on the scale, and 3) eat better since I'm not exercising. Small steps I began to find myself taking were things like not getting milkshakes at Cookout, making a billion cookies around the holiday's but eating almost none of them, and cutting out (or at least trying to cut out) all bread because bread is bad and the ultimate source to all weight gain. Wait. Maybe that's just what I believed. In taking these steps, my weight resulted in a fluctuating between 114 and 116 pounds.

The steps I was taking seemed completely normal and not at all dangerous to my body; it was my thought process behind my actions that was dangerous to my body. My motives slowly became kryptic to me, and I never did realize these effects. Any time I ate anything that was "unhealthy," like any dessert foods for instance, I instantly felt guilty. I would feel regret and shame about one choice of a meal for the whole day and sometimes even the next day.

March... Bathing Suits and Beaches

Then, March came around, which meant spring break which meant THE BEACH. I went to the beach with my best friend. After being in swimsuits the whole week, my insecurities increased. I came back from vacation and began taking steps towards a "better looking body." Now, not only was my motive to see the number drop on the scale, but also to have a flat tummy (which I'm pretty sure my stomach couldn't get any flatter than it already was) and visible abs. My motives turned into physical appearance-driven motives. And I'm going to be completely honest here, these new motives were definitely encouraged and influenced by an increased intake of social media. By constantly going on social media, I looked at the images of other girls my age and wanted my body to look just the same. I followed fitness accounts and accounts of nutritionists. The body these girls had intimidated me, and motivated me even more to have that flat tummy full of abs. And if I'm being even more honest, I looked to Pinterest for workouts to do and foods to eat that would give me the body I was idolizing. After heavy investigation (literally), I applied only a few things that I learned, to my life. I occasionally went on runs and constantly found myself doing exercises to give me the abs I so desperately wanted. Not at all was I pursuing any set or consistent exercise plan. My "plan" was to exercise whenever I felt like it, and whenever I felt "fat." This meant that checking my image in the mirror became a pretty regular thing for me. After only a few weeks of trying, nothing seemed to be working. I didn't put full effort into achieving this goal, nor did I spend enough time trying, so obviously abs were not going to just magically appear like I had hoped.

April 2016... Guidelines

A lack of patience was something that I had developed and I let it affect me throughout this time in my life. Eventually, my lack of patience resulted in a different method, or way of lifestyle. This new method was restriction. I restricted my meals, snacks, and the food I ate. And I guess you could say I set "guidelines," being: 3 small meals, every 4 hours. I didn't count or track my calories, but I checked the calories on products, and if it seemed to be too much, I just wouldn't eat it. For breakfast, I almost always had a small portion of greek yogurt with fruit and granola, and then a cup of green tea. My choice of beverage was ALWAYS coffee, but after hearing that green tea was a good metabolism-booster (aka "fat burner," I thought), I transitioned to tea. Almost every other meal I ate was a salad or fruits, veggies, and meat. If I wanted tuna, having it on bread or crackers wasn't an option, so tuna on cucumbers became the new regime. Under these self imposed regulations sandwiches weren't much of an option. What I didn't realize was that carbs are actually necessary, and I wasn't consuming any.. In fact, it went like this... Mamma made pasta, I refused to ate it, and made my own meal. Mamma made chicken, a veggie, and rice; I ate the chicken and veggies. Almost always did I find myself refusing to eat at least one thing my Mom put in front of me, kind of forcing her to always make sure there was an abundance of items in the fridge for me to be able to make a salad. How boring, right? Salads for every meal. LAME. And you also may be wondering what dining out looked like for me. Eating at restaurants meant salads or grilled lean meat, and occasionally sandwiches (lettuce as bread). Which, let me just tell you, I enjoy my sandwiches either way, bread or lettuce, but never did I once allow myself to have that bread.

Honestly, I didn't see any problems with this way of living. I truly thought that my body was physically unattractive and in order to fix it, I pretty much just needed to starve myself. This was my thought process: shed the fat off, and you'll be able to see abs. Which I realize now is a distorted and incorrect way of thinking. Not only was I starving myself, but I was depriving my body of the nutrients it needed. Another problem with this lifestyle, was the emotions behind my motives, and the way I thought of myself. I was insecure in every way. This was not at all what God wanted for me or designed for me. It wasn't until a few months into this lifestyle that I realized this though.

July 2016… Coming to Terms with God's Gracious Love

The last week of July I went with my church, Newspring, on the annual beach camp trip, Gauntlet, for my sixth year in a row. This is, and always has been, my favorite week of summer. At Gauntlet, I experience Jesus on my level, through worship and sermons, and even get to have a little fun in the Florida weather. This specific Gauntlet though, was different. Every part about it made my soul completely on fire for Jesus. Most importantly, it created a change in me, that would impact my life and other's lives when I returned. This Gauntlet, I let go of the insecurities that were holding me captive. I realized I had a problem. I confessed the problem to my leader and my dearest cousin. This all happened Wednesday night; we had just heard a powerful message, God was speaking right to me. He wasn't just speaking to me though, the sermon weighed heavy on all our hearts and as soon as we got back to our hotel room everyone had something to share. We sat in a circle and began sharing. I sat there listening to everybody's stories, in complete awe at what God was doing. Finally, it was my turn. I shared a few things on my mind, but I was holding back the most important secret I had.

A few girls were slowly falling asleep. The stories were shared. Everybody was in their own world. It was in that moment that I leaned over to my cousin and whispered in her ear, "I have another thing to share." She sat there ready and open to what I had to say. So I went for it. And as the words came out of my mouth, I cried. Then of course, she cried. And there we were, both crying. She wrapped her arms around me and just held me. I realized, this was the peace that I so desperately needed and was searching for.

During this moment I felt like we were the only ones in the room, but my small group leader knew we weren't. After seeing us in tears, she joined in the moment. I let her in on the "secret." Being the great leader and human being that she is, she began pouring wisdom and most importantly, love, into me. Just like that, there we were, all three of us, just crying. Once the tears died down, and we could all form words with our mouths… they spoke truth into me. They reassured me that I didn't have to live this way anymore. They instilled a peace and feeling of rest in me. Finally. It was so evident that love and comfort was in the air. Not only their love, but God's love. This is what living with Jesus looks like..

I left Gauntlet 2016 not only on fire for Jesus and his people, but in love with myself and my body because my image is found in God and God alone. No longer did I have to discourage myself. The scale didn't define me, nor did the mirror's reflection. Finally, I knew that I was beautifully and wonderfully made by the creator of the universe (Psalm 139:14).

When I returned home, I didn't tell my family members. I knew it was what I had to do, but I wasn't ready to announce. And if I'm being honest, part of me still thought it wasn't that big of a problem, and I could come up out of it alone. I figured as long as I told at least one person, I was in the clear. This was not the case. I needed somebody in my home to help me and to guide me. Soon enough, that help came. That help was my parents- through my sister's tattle-tale self. Sisters. They know when something's wrong, it's like some sixth sense or something. A sixth sense that my sister apparently has, because she knew I wasn't okay and she knew she had to let my parents know, so she did. And contrary to what you may think, I am eternally grateful to her for doing so.

August 2016... No Turning Back

Only a short week or two after the Gauntlet I got a call from my Mom that an appointment was scheduled with my pediatrician. She told me not to fear. And she also told me that my doctor would be checking my health status. Was this real? Had it reached this point? These were a few things I wondered. Okay, I'm sorry, I thought I had this under control. I thought doing this alone was smart. Psych. God knew I couldn't do this alone and He made sure that exactly these sequence of events would happen. Was I mad you ask? Surprisingly no. I knew I needed to let my Mom in on this secret, and somehow I was relieved of the pressure to do so. God ALWAYS knows what He's doing, in case you didn't know.

So on the Monday afternoon of my appointment my Mom, Dad, and I walked into the Greenville Children's Medical Center. We were called back to a room. First, they weighed me, with my back turned. This was the procedure for cases like mine. In this moment I remember feeling completely awestruck. I was shocked. I was partially scared. How had I reached this point? This question continued to pop up in my head. Without realizing it, my life would be changed from this point on. This day- a turning point. Hiding in this lifestyle wasn't an option anymore. People know now. No turning back.

Moments later my doctor met my family, back in the room. I remember her showing concern for me, to my face. And when she asked me how I was doing, what was going on, I had no response. What WAS going on? What was I supposed to say? That I was starving myself? I didn't really know what kind of response she was looking for, so my Dad took the wheel. He explained the circumstances. He explained his concern for me, and my Mom's concern for me. And I just sat there. I allowed his responses to wash over me, because he cared. I could see the love he had for me, his daughter, and I was comforted. It was almost like, in a way, my Dad was telling me everything was okay and I didn't have to feel embarrassed or shy about the circumstances I was going through. Having this strong support system was and is important when coming to the realization that I came to. Having a support system like this carried me through the day, and through the days to come.

My doctor, a freaking killer woman in fact, shared equal concern. She spoke from a medical standpoint, deeper than my Dad's. It was through her response, that my parents discovered I had dropped 9 pounds in weight since my last check-up in March. From March to August, I had lost nine pounds. Being that my original weight was on the lower end of average in the first place, this was pretty concerning to her. The first question she asked me after sharing this fact was, "When was your last period?" April was my last period. Through sharing this, she brought up a point I had never thought, nor had my parents. And that was- the loss of weight I was experiencing, did in fact, affect my menstrual cycle. So now, not only was I underweight, but I wasn't having a period, and this was very concerning to her.

The first thing she recommended was meeting with a nutritionist/therapist. As these words came out of her mouth, my Mom began to cry. She turned to me, confirming that that was what I wanted to do. We both sat there crying and what came into my head once again was, "Had it really reached this point?"

I realized something at that moment. Although my Mom was crying, they weren't tears of embarrassment or disappointment. No. That's not my Mom. Her tears were tears of deep care for me. She never said the words, but I knew she was sorry. I knew that she couldn't believe it had reached this point either and she was sorry she hadn't noticed. Not only that, but she was sorry that I had felt this way. She hated that I felt this way, that my feelings about myself had come to these circumstances. Never would she ever wish this on her children, and to sit there and see me going through this pain and conflict with myself, it hurt her. She's a great woman, my Mamma. It was through her support also that I was able to make it through that day. Her tender love and care kept me stable.

We left the appointment that day, with a feeling that everything was going to be okay. I was going to get through this, and so would my parents. And my parents would be there the whole way to make sure of it.

Keep on Keepin On

A week later we did it all over again. The procedures were the same. We checked my weight. We talked about how I was feeling. Everything went the same, but I felt different. A change started to develop in me. Slowly, I started to feel a little more confident about myself and my body image. This wasn't because of some magic performed by the doctor or my parents although their love did encourage me to keep on, keepin on. It was Jesus. Through confession to the people who mean most in my life and through my relationship with Jesus, I felt secure. I felt peace. I'm a strong believer that with Jesus, anything is possible. Jesus wouldn't give you tough circumstances to endure if He didn't think you could make it through them and come up out of them stronger than before. Which is why I was in these circumstances and also why I was making it. Jesus was my rock and my foundation through all of this. I wasn't awesome or some crazy confident girl, no that's not the case. I just had Jesus. That's all you need.

October... Living a God Designed Life

Today, only a couple months later, as I am writing about these past struggles, I am writing from a perspective of redemption. The Lord has redeemed me and continues to redeem me from every bit of struggle, every day. Through every moment spent in the Word, through every moment spent at church learning about God's great love for me, through every moment worshipping the Greatest love, and through every moment I spend with God's people, I experience redemption and freedom.

Now, I want to live a healthy lifestyle. Now, I want to make sure I am treating my body with the tender love and care that is needs. Not only do I want to do this for me physically, but for me mentally and spiritually. By living a healthy lifestyle, I will be at a healthy weight, I will have a regular menstrual cycle, and will have sustaining energy. By treating my body right and loving it, like I am called to, I can rest in my feelings about my image. I can have peace in the fact that God created me. He thinks I am beautiful. Psalm 139:14 says "I praise you, for I am fearfully and wonderfully made. Wonderful are your works; my soul knows it very well." The Lord put thought into creating me; He made my image wonderful. I knew I had to honor God with my body. By restricting my diet and looking at my body in a negative way, I was not praising God for giving me this body, nor was I honoring God with my body. In 1 Corinthians 6:19-20 Paul says, "Or do you not know that your body is a temple of the Holy Spirit within you, whom you have from God? You are not your own, for you were bought with a price. So glorify God in your body." I am called, as a Christian, to glorify God in my body. My body is a temple, given to me. I need to take care of this gift. Through both of these verses, I was able to realize that to pursue a healthy lifestyle, meant I was obeying God and his calling for my life. And every step of obedience towards God leads to growth in my relationship with God. Ultimately, I knew that if I wanted to grow in my relationship with Jesus, I would have to accept what God was calling me to do, and that was to stop dishonoring my body. It was time for me to give it to Him, give it all to Him. In return, I would receive rest. So I gave my struggles to God, and slowly He has been redeeming me.

Of course, I still have negative thoughts in regard to my physical appearance. Occasionally I catch myself looking in the mirror and having the desire to change things about my physical appearance . Yes I still stand on that scale every once in awhile. And yes, I still have feelings of regret after overeating or even eating something I know isn't healthy for my body. Most importantly though, these feelings don't drive my behavior anymore. I push past those feelings and I look to what Jesus says about me and what He calls me to do. If you want to overcome issues with eating, you have to look past what you feel and past what your flesh desires, and look to what God has to offer. What He has to offer is far greater than anything your flesh or the world can try and offer you. He offers immeasurably more.

Health in God's Eyes

By laying this groundwork of how God created me, and you too, I also need to share, what He says about living healthy, and eating healthy.

In Proverbs 23:20-21 Jesus says, "Be not among drunkards or among gluttonous eaters of meat," specifically telling us not to over-drink or overeat. Gluttony is the word Jesus uses to make this demand.

Then, in Exodus 20: 3-5 Jesus also says, "You shall have no other gods before me. You shall not make for yourself a carved image, or any likeness of anything that is in heaven above, or that is in the earth beneath, or that is in the water under the earth. You shall not bow down to them or serve them, for I the Lord your God am a jealous God."

In both of these verses we see God giving His people specific commands to life a healthy lifestyle. As a part of living healthy, you should not overeat or undereat, both are disobeying God. Overeating and undereating both create idols in your life, in which God calls you directly not to honor. Overeating creates an idol of food. If you are relying on food to please you, you are not relying on God to please you. In other words, finding pleasure in food is putting food above God. Undereating, on the other hand, also creates an idol higher than God. Under-eating, or restricting your diet for the worse, which is what I was doing, is putting yourself in control. You see, by restricting myself, I was saying, "I am in control of my life. This is my body and I am going to treat it how I want, even if it is not God's best for me." I was creating a carved image for myself, my body image, my physical appearance. Never was I looking to what God thought of me, or to how God wanted me to live. I was living purely for my own selfish ambitions and wants.

Living either of these lifestyles not only has a negative effect on your body physically, but also have a negative effect on your body mentally and emotionally. And therefore, have a negative effect on you spiritually. You see, God has a purpose for each and every one of us. That purpose can be looked at in a broad sense- to carry the Gospel to the world.

"Therefore go and make disciples of all nations, baptizing them in the name of the Father and of the Son and of the Holy Spirit, and teaching them to obey everything I have commanded you. And surely I am with you always, to the very end of the age." Matthew 28:19-20.

And that purpose can also be looked at in a narrow sense- how God wants to use you in every area of your life (at school, work, friendships, relationships).

For me, I realized that I am called by God to carry the Gospel to everyone I come in contact with. Right now, for me, that means my school. My school is my mission field, and Bible studies on Thursday mornings is just one of the ways I am living out that purpose. But my first priority, was taking care of myself the way God wanted me to. If I wanted to reach out to God's people, I needed to make sure I was healthy: physically, mentally, and spiritually.

As Christians, each and every one of us need to treat our bodies right, for ourselves and for God. Physical health is important to God, which is why it should be important to you too. So get out there and move. Go on a run. Do some yoga. And if you're me, stock up on a billion jars of Wild Friends peanut butter, because why not?

Distorted Beauty .... Chapter 2

"You are altogether beautiful my darling; there is no flaw in you."

Song of Solomon 4:7

As you read about my past in the previous chapter, you may have realized my underlying problem. I have/had an eating disorder. This was a reality of mine that I denied for months and still to this day am shocked to believe. Regardless of my shock, I chose to accept it. I chose to accept the truth because I knew that was the first step to healing AND eternal health. After all, God wants me to be the best me that I can be, and that means physical health too, ladies.

In this chapter I will address the different eating disorders and the features that fall under them. (My goal is to provide you with information I was clueless about) Maybe you're like me and an eating disorder is an underlying problem that you have never thought about or possibly thought about and kept to yourself. On the other hand, maybe you do not relate to disorders, but rather have a friend or family member who does. Regardless of your situation, I believe every teenage girl should be educated on the extreme reality of eating disorders. According to a study done by the National Association of Anorexia Nervosa and Associated Disorders (ANAD), at least 30 million people of all ages and genders suffer from an eating disorder in the United States[1].

IMPORTANT: As you read through the different disorders, remember this truth: "You are altogether beautiful my darling; there is no flaw in you." Song of Solomon 4:7. You are not defined by a basic medical definition. You are defined by the Creator of the Universe and that definition is beautiful.

Anorexia Nervosa

Anorexia Nervosa, often times, has a bad connotation by the public. Unfortunately, it's used as a negative reference towards young males and females. Boys may toss around the word to their "bros," calling them anorexic because their muscles aren't big enough or their legs are too skinny, then laugh it off like it's some joke. Girls can even be engaged in the same type of behavior. Shocker, right? As we all know, girls can be cruel. (Where do you think the idea for the movie *Mean Girls* came from?) Exhibit A- calling another girl anorexic because she's skinnier than you or has long thin legs- that's cruel. Since when did anorexia become normal locker room talk? And when did it become an okay word to throw around at your friends?

Reality is, anorexia is a serious issue. Not many understand the severity of it because of society's failure as a whole to portray the importance of the issue. So I think it's time for me to share the importance and the deepest realities that many are clueless about.

Diagnostic Criteria

According to the Diagnostic and Statistical Manual of Mental Disorders 5th edition (DSM-V), there are three diagnostic criteria for Anorexia Nervosa[2]:

1. Restriction of energy intake relative to requirement, leading to a significantly low body weight in the context of age, sex, developmental trajectory, and physical health.
2. Intense fear of gaining weight or becoming fat, or persistent behavior that interferes with weight gain, even though at a significantly low weight.

3. Disturbance in the way in which one's body weight or shape is experienced, undue influence of body weight or shape on self-evaluation, or persistent lack of recognition of the seriousness of the current low body weight.

Effects of the Symptoms

When people think of anorexia, they can usually point out the characteristics easily. We all have a general idea of what anorexia looks like, whether we realize it or not. Something that not many of us think about though, are the dangers and lifetime effects of anorexia on a human's life. Anorexia creates concerns in two major areas: the digestive system and the reproductive system[2].

As a result of fearing weight gain and becoming fat, many women will literally starve themselves to death. Which is the very scary and dangerous part not many think of; anorexia can result in death when our bodies are not getting the nutrients they need to maintain, grow, and feed our inner organs.

Anorexia also creates concern in the reproductive system of our bodies[3]. This may come as a shock to many, because it sure did come as a huge shocker to me. I remember sitting in my doctor's office back in August and my doctor asked me, "When was the last time you had your period?" After seeing the concerned looked she had on her face when I said March, I realized that the decisions I had been making in my life the past few months had in fact, affected my overall health. And that's exactly how it can affect you- a loss of menstruation for at least three cycles in a row[3]. Restricting your body from the nutrients it needs, can eventually create a hormonal imbalance; your body stops producing estrogen- a vital hormone for maintaining the menstrual cycle- and in result, causes your body to stop having a regular cycle[3].

Bulimia Nervosa

Bulimia is also a very dangerous eating disorder affecting 1.5% of women in America, as shown in the same study by ANAD[1]. Many of us may have seen this disorder portrayed in a movie or tv show (which always fails to portray it completely correct) or maybe some of us have seen it play out in the lives of people around us, but I doubt very many of you have. And the reason for that is bulimia is a very distinct disorder, hard to notice in another's life. Contrary to victims of other eating disorders, victims of bulimia nervosa tend to maintain or *control* their weight, and physical appearance. Victims do not starve themselves, but rather the quite opposite- they binge eat (on anything and everything) past the point of being full. Then, in order to control their weight, they act in compensatory behaviors to empty out all of the bad calories. Victims are concerned with gaining more weight, so they may purge, over-exercise, or set crazy restrictions, to avoid it the weight gain.

Diagnostic Criteria

According to the DSM-V, there are five diagnostic criteria for Bulimia Nervosa[4]:
1. Recurrent episodes of binge eating.
2. Recurrent inappropriate compensatory behaviors (self-induced vomiting, misuse of laxatives, fasting, or excessive exercise) in order to prevent weight gain.

3. The binge eating and inappropriate compensatory behaviors both occur, on average, at least 1 time a week for at least 3 months.
4. Self-evaluation is unduly influenced by body shape and weight.
5. The disturbance does not occur exclusively during episodes of anorexia nervosa.

Effects of Symptoms

Unfortunately, bulimia, just like anorexia, can have very serious affects on the human body. Not only does bulimia prevent the body from receiving its daily dietary needs, but also causes much danger to the internal organs. Many people are unaware of this outcome, which is why I believe it is so important to be informed of the physical effects and ultimately, the dangers they have on the body.

First, let's talk about the effects bulimia has on the digestive system. Purging and vomiting causes tooth decay, an inflamed (or even torn) esophagus, and swollen salivary gland. Further in the digestive system, purging from bulimia can cause ruptures or tears in the stomach and problems with the bowels. Also, because all food and water consumed is being released through purging, the body fails to receive any nutrients or water to support another important system, the cardiovascular system. Victim's bodies become prone to dehydration, a low body temperature, and a loss of consciousness since the body's blood levels are low due to the lack proper nourishment[4].

Binge-Eating

Binge-eating is an eating disorder on the opposite end of the eating disorder spectrum, causing many people to fail to recognize it. In fact, it wasn't until the Diagnostic and Statistical Manual for Mental Disorders (DSM) was updated, that we found binge eating disorder (BED) being defined. Unfortunately, binge eating disorder is the most common eating disorder, affecting 2.8% of American adults[1]. Not only is binge eating hard to recognize, but also very hard to control. Just like with bulimia, victims of BED binge on outrageous amounts of food, past the point of being full. Victims will literally eat everything in sight until they can physically not eat anymore. Unlike bulimia though, victims of this disorder do not participate in compensatory behaviors to rid of the excessive food and calorie consumption. This means binge-eating victims are typically overweight or obese.

Diagnostic Criteria

[5]According to the DSM-V, there are
1. Recurrent and persistent episodes of binge eating
2. Binge eating episodes are associated with three (or more) of the following:
   a. Eating much more rapidly than normal
   b. Eating until feeling uncomfortably full
   c. Eating large amounts of food when not feeling physically hungry
   d. Eating alone because of being embarrassed by how much one is eating
   e. Feeling disgusted with oneself, depressed, or very guilty after overeating

3. Marked distress regarding binge eating
4. Absence of regular compensatory behaviors (such as purging).

Effects of Symptoms

Most people with binge-eating disorder, end up obese or in a state closely related to it. Just as with obesity, they may experience serious medical problems including: high cholesterol, high blood pressure, diabetes, gallbladder disease, and/or heart disease[5]. In the end, the effects of binge-eating end up *limiting* the quantity and quality of foods patients can consume. Ultimately, binge-eating backfires on the human body.

Orthorexia

Orthorexia, also known as "a fixation on righteous eating," is a fairly new disorder being addressed by doctors and nutritionists. As of lately, it is not in the DSM-V or described formally as a medical condition, but does seem to be looked at as an important medical issue by medical professionals. People with orthorexia tend to be obsessed with the "healthiness" of their food, rather than the amount of food they eat, as with people with anorexia. In other words, patients with anorexia obsess over restriction of all foods, while patients with orthorexia obsess over restriction of all unhealthy foods.

Doctors describe orthorexia with a few symptoms[6]:
1. Spending frequent amounts of time thinking about healthy food
2. Not enjoying the food they eat
3. Limiting the number of foods they eat

4. Cannot eat anywhere but at home
5. Criticize other's "bad" eating habits
6. Feeling full of guilt and regret when they eat "bad" foods
7. Refusing to indulge in foods they love

Effects of Symptoms

For those who struggle with orthorexia, their desire to live a healthy lifestyle eventually turns into an all-out attempt to live a "perfect" healthy lifestyle. What started out as striving to only eat healthy foods, eventually creates restriction in not only the quality of foods, but in the quantity too. Their desire to be healthy completely backfires. Pretty ironic right? The choices they pushed to create healthy habits, end up in fact, creating *more* unhealthy habits than they had before. In the end, victims of orthorexia suffer and ultimately, so does their health.

Physically, their body suffers from the lack of variety in their diet and from the lack of calories needed to nourish, grow, and thrive. Mentally, they suffer from the lack of not only brain-enhancing nutrients, but also socialization and community. You see, because of the desire to eat clean by eating at home, they are isolating themselves from social situations. Rather than getting out of the house and going out to eat with a close friend, people with orthorexia would rather turn down the opportunity and cook at home to ensure they are not eating anything "bad" for the body. Many times, you see their relationships falling apart and disappearing, as they begin to put food on a pedestal, at top priority.

Real Life

This is where my life comes in. After going to the doctor in August, to discuss the restrictive diet I had put myself on over the past few months, I decided I needed to change my lifestyle. So, August 2016 I made the decision to start making healthy decisions for my life and my body. I began intentionally eating my food, at meal times and between meals when I was hungry. I began to listen to my body, unlike ever before. As I began to research and learn about what a healthy lifestyle looks like, I incorporated some of those ideas into my daily routine. I followed more food bloggers and their lifestyles. Then, slowly but surely, I started to slip down another unhealthy path.

The end of November hit and I was in this feeling of being trapped AGAIN. I thought to myself, What happened?! It wasn't until January that I realized I had become obsessed with pursuing a healthy lifestyle. In fact, my constant pursuit to live this way was restricting my life in ways I hadn't realized. My relationships were fading away, I didn't care. I became distant from my church community, I didn't care. I stopped pouring into my small group, my community, and even my relationship with Jesus. Honestly, living the perfect life and having a healthy relationship with food just seemed so much better than going to that unhealthy restaurant with my group of friends. How my body felt and how it looked was so much more important to me than the group of friends that were in my circle, and I didn't even realize that these thoughts were buried deep in my subconscious.

Although I may have realized this in January, it took me until February to begin knocking these walls down and living a life of freedom. You see, freedom was a series of new steps, growth, and ongoing life-change. So what was so special about February?

On February 18th, I flew down to Haiti on a mission trip with a group of my closest friends and most importantly, my loving Father. Prior to going on this trip, I was scared, uncomfortable, and SO. NOT. EXCITED. "Whaaat?!" I know! I was going to freaking Haiti! Why was I not completely EXHILARATED. Well, honestly, I was too overwhelmed and focused on the food aspect of the trip, that I blocked out every exciting thing I was about to experience. Food was on my pedestal, my top priority.

February 18th, these walls were torn down. Our team arrived in Haiti and enjoyed our first meal in the home we would be staying at for the week. After discussing what the week would look like and realizing I would be eating foods WAY out of my "healthy standards," I began to panic. In fact, I was screaming inside. My head felt like it was going to explode with everything that I was filling it with. All I wanted to do was burst into a billion tears, right there at the dinner table, in front of everyone.

My Dad, being that he *is* my Dad and can tell when *anything* is wrong, could sense the complete fear just by the look on my face. He pulled me aside in the kitchen that night and poured the most encouraging words into me that I believe came straight from God, through him, and to me. Instantly, peace flushed over me. God was in that moment.

By the next day, I was completely dependent on God. In fact, no longer was food my top priority. Jesus was my top priority. Jesus was on my pedestal. And no, I'm not just saying this, this is legit. Our second night there, the mother of the home set out beef in the crockpot and mashed potatoes in front of us. Okay first, I don't eat red meat, haven't eaten it in almost 2 years. Second, I have always refused to eat mashed potatoes because of the "unhealthy" vibe they have given off. And there I was, sitting at a table in front of both of those foods. God was clearly trying to a) be funny and b) teach me something.

I ate the whole dang meal. What were the results? No fear. No guilt. No regret. In fact, immediately after eating this meal (which yes, was very delicious) I asked God for peace that night. Being the great God he is, he gave me immediate peace and best of all, *joy.* I remember telling my dear friend the next afternoon, "Just in the two days we have been here, I have had more joy than I have had in the last few months. It's so crazy, I feel so different. I feel like my mindset and attitude has completely changed just in two days."

Her response to me? "I can see it Nicole! I was going to say the same thing! I have seen such a difference in you since we've been here!"

God works miracles- miracles you would never expect him to work. Going into Haiti, I felt chained. I didn't think I was going to make it through the week. In fact, if you would have talked to me before, I probably would have told you that I thought I was going to die from that one week of "bad" eating. Well guess what friends? I didn't die! I survived. Not only did I come out of that week alive; I came out of that week *set free.* The chains were broken and I was in God-designed FREEDOM.

Isn't it crazy what God will do to get us to realize He is the only way? God had to get me all the way to Haiti just for me to realize that I couldn't live on food alone. In order for me to thrive, grow, and flourish in my life, I needed to live on God.

I left that week with a new outlook on my life and the things that should matter most to me. I left with a growing relationship with Jesus and a whole new type of love for Him. I left with a rekindled relationship with all of my friends who I had mistakenly distanced myself from over the past few months. Lastly, I created a new relationship with food. This new relationship? A relationship without restriction. I created a relationship of balance. Now, I strive for a healthy life with my body and growing love for the body God gave me.

Just like me, there are girls everywhere who have dealt with the same circumstances. Some of those girls have been set free and can live a life of redemption and unfortunately, some (maybe even you) are still living a life trapped in darkness. Fortunately, I have had the opportunity to communicate with a few women in my life who have undergone similar circumstances and even better, have been set FREE...

Stories of Redemption .... Chapter 3

"Therefore confess your sins to each other and pray for each other so that you may be healed. The prayer of a righteous person is powerful and effective."

James 5:16

Maybe you're struggling with an eating disorder, or an unhealthy relationship with food that hasn't quite reached the point it could be classified as an "eating disorder." You feel completely alone. You feel like nobody understands what you are going through or the pain you are enduring. I understand how you feel because that's how I felt and that's how the girls in these stories I am about to share, feel. Each of these girls hold a special position of importance in my life. They have impacted my life in different ways through their stories. This is evidence that we can learn a lot from paths other people walk and how Jesus worked through their lives. That is why I wanted to share their stories with you. Here we go...

Ryan

The story you are about to read is from Ryan. I met this beautiful girl my Sophomore year of high school and it wasn't until my Senior year that we became friends. We began leading a group called Girl's Committed to Christ (GCTC), where we studied the Bible and created the deep relationships with girls at my school. It was through this opportunity that I got the chance to meet Ryan and get to know more about her story and her relationship with Jesus. I believe the Lord planted this friendship in my life at just the exact time I needed it. (It's funny how He works, isn't it?)

Here are a few things Ryan believes you need to know about her, and even about yourself,

"The hardest thing I've ever experienced was having an eating disorder, but I would go through it all again to be who I am today. For close to a year, every single day was a struggle. I remember crying every morning, having thoughts of food and exercise completely control my thoughts, and losing all of my friends because I wouldn't hang out with anyone. I was cranky and mean and weak from not eating and if I missed a workout I would literally lay down on the floor and cry so much I couldn't physically get back up. I wanted to die every day. I felt pretty far away from God for awhile until my mom told me one day that I didn't have to be perfect to come to God (I also struggle with perfection). I could just come to him and tell him that I needed help. So that's what I did. My eating disorder didn't go away and neither did my depression because those aren't sins or little dips in your mood, they're diseases of the mind and that's ok. But as I went forward I knew I had God on my side. It forced me to trust him more and see that I had never trusted him like this before. If you're reading the Bible right now in the middle of an ED and think it's pointless, you're not alone. I was so overwhelmed with life I had to take the Bible step by step and just read a chapter or a few verses each day. Some verses that helped me were:

1 Corinthians 3:22-23, "For God has already given you everything you need... He has given you the whole world to use, and life and even death are your servants. He has given you all of the present and all of the future. All are yours, and you belong to Christ, and Christ is God's." You have all you need to recover.

1 Corinthians 6:19-20, "Haven't you yet learned that your body is the home of the Holy Spirit God gave you, and that he lives within you? Your own body does not belong to you. For God has bought you with a great price. So use every part of your body to give glory back to God, because he owns it."

2 Corinthians 4:16-18, "That is why we never give up. Though our bodies are dying, our inner strength in the Lord is growing every day. These troubles and sufferings of ours are, after all, quite small and won't last very long. Yet this short time of distress will result in God's richest blessing upon us forever and ever! So, we do not look at what we can see right now, the troubles all around us, but we look

forward to the joys in heaven which we have not yet seen. The troubles will soon be over, but the joys to come will last forever." (I think about heaven a lot)

My favorite teacher and someone who has become a great influence in my life told me this verse when I first told him about my eating disorder: Ecclesiastes 7:14 "When times are good, be happy; but when times are bad consider this: God has made the one as well as the other." also 7:18 "Whoever fears God will avoid extremes."

We have to realize that God has given us the bad times as well as the good. Plus, eating disorders are all about going to the extremes and we can remember that God wants us to be in the middle.

You probably feel like you'll never recover. I know I did and sometimes I still wonder if it will ever fully go away. But when I look back to two years ago to when I was first diagnosed to where I am now it's like a different person, and not just in my eating habits and depression. My personality has come back and changed a little. I have immense respect for myself and demand it from others which led me away from the people I was hanging out with who took advantage of me, to finding the two best friends I've ever had. I stopped liking the boy who treated me like crap. I started standing up for myself. I never thought I'd get to where am I today and it's honestly because of therapy, medicine, and of course God. So don't ever be ashamed or afraid of needing help. I know God gave me this for a reason and as much as it sucked and continues to be a struggle for me, I don't regret the path God has led me down. It's made me a new person, given me a testimony to share with others, strengthened my relationship with God and my family, and has led me to some amazing people including the author of this book.

Lastly, I'll leave you with my favorite verse and one I've clung to for the past almost 3 years now. Romans 8:28: "And we know that in all things, God works together for the good of those who love Him."[1]

Haley

Another lady whose story I have had the chance to get to know is Haley. Haley is a food blogger I followed on Instagram after seeing her beautiful and inspiring posts on the Instagram explore page. Once I stalked her Instagram for a little (okay don't act like that's a weird thing to do, I know all of you do it), I became hooked and HAD to subscribe to her blog, Hungry Haley. I began reading her blog and enjoying her different recipes. So, as any normal teenager would do, I decided to contact her. We chatted about food blogging and this book.

Upon searching through her blog, I found a post on her story and her experience with an eating disorder. After reading this post, I remember feeling encouraged. I was encouraged to pursue a healthy lifestyle for myself and I was encouraged to share my story with others, including people who I do not know. Because her story had such an impact on me, I asked her if I could share it with you. So here it is...

"Between July and August of 2012, I started losing weight. Sure, the compliments were great – "Wow, you look thin!" and "What have you been up to, girl? You're so toned!" – things like that. *Fitness* Magazines piled up on my desk, and my parents made room in the kitchen for me to experiment with new healthy recipes I'd found. I was even performing well in school – I was studying constantly and rewarded with several A's. My faith was strong, too. I read my bible, connected with my bible-study leader at the time, Jessica, and spent time in God's word.

But things headed downhill when I lost some control. My friends would all go out for dinner and a movie and I'd politely decline. I convinced all of us (myself, my friends, and my parents) that it was because I had homework and wanted to save money, but I knew that, honestly, it was because I was afraid to eat unhealthy food.

That was strike 1.

After school everyday, (yes, every single day) I'd head over to the gym for a good, sweaty 45 minutes on the stair-climber and then some mileage on the treadmill. Everyday. Afterwards, I'd shower, steam some veggies and pair it with lean meat like chicken, turkey, or pork, and hit the books for the rest of the night, forgetting about family dinners and unintentionally lighting the match that would begin to char away the thick ropes that tied our relationship together.

That was strike 2.

Soon enough, my breakfast was one egg and a few whites scrambled with spinach, and a banana with peanut butter. My lunch bag held nothing but half a turkey sandwich, carrots, and an apple. And my eating habits only became more and more strict from there. I wasn't quite aware of it, but something was grabbing a hold of the reigns in my life.

And there is strike 3.

February of 2013 was the first turning point of many. My heart pounded with fear when my mom told me she scheduled a doctor's appointment for me. Our family doctor is one of the sweetest, most genuine, caring women I've ever met, yet I dreaded this appointment more than anything. I think she knew what was going on before the appointment, even though I thought it was just a check-up. First, she told me I was underweight by almost 10 pounds. Then, she began asking personal questions like why I stayed at home so often, why my grades were so high all of a sudden, why I wasn't on the track team, etc. And then she and my mom brain-stormed answers they assumed (and read to be) true to all those questions – answers I knew were true, but didn't want to admit. Tears filled my eyes and everything my doctor said after "You have an eating disorder" was a blur. I remember hearing something about needing therapy, too… That story is nowhere near over. In fact, more and more is added to it everyday. A little part of me hesitates to admit that I had an eating disorder, but I would never wish it hadn't happened. God showed me that He can be weird, and often misunderstood, but He can never be wrong. He will never allow anything, anyone, or any trial tear you down. I'm trusting Him and learning more and more about Him, this life He's blessed me with, and the food that comes with it every single day[2].

Lauren

I've known Lauren for quite some time. I first met her in seventh grade. It was one night after Fuse, my youth ministry, that I realized my small group was falling apart. Well I don't know if you would call me and a leader a small group. I wasn't involved in the community that God wanted me involved in. As a result, I wasn't growing spiritually the way that God desires for each and every one of us. I knew it was time to look for a new small group… and this is where Lauren came in. Lauren was 19 at the time, leading a large group of girls who were a year older than me. I joined her group and they quickly welcomed me with glad and sincere hearts. Something in me confirmed, this was where I belonged.

Ever since that day in seventh grade, I have been a part of Lauren's small group. We have been huge parts of each other's lives. I've gone to her wedding and ONE DAY

she will go to mine. (All the giddy feelings saying that).
She's helped me through the toughest of circumstances-
breakups, friendship issues, and even now as I face the
effects of an eating disorder. When I look at her I
immediately think, "She's a difference maker."

Having her as my small group leader doesn't just
mean that I get to share my life with her. Our relationship
works both ways, and that's what I love so much about it. It
shows God's purpose for community. I get to dump my life
on her and she gets to dump her life on me. Hehe. So, since
we have this equal relationship with each other, I have gotten
to know a whole lot about her over the years. Lately though,
she has let me into her life just a little bit more.
In fact, it was at our beach camp last year (summer of 2016)
that she shared with me her unhealthy relationship with food.
She had been struggling and needed somebody to walk with
her and encourage her through these struggles. Not only was
I so thankful for her courage to confess this me, but my heart
was also set at ease because I was also struggling with an
unhealthy relationship with food at the time. Her sharing her
story was not only good for her heart, but equally as good for
my heart- which, of course, was God's plan.

When I began writing this part of my book and I
began to think about all of the stories I wanted to include in
this section, I thought of Lauren. Why? Because her story
comes from a different perspective and a different
background than the rest. Here it is…

"Let me just start by saying that I was raised in the
country with all the fixin's! Literally I ate so many
casseroles, biscuits, sweets and few veggies (most of which
were mixed in the casseroles or from a can). I also hated
fruit, I was super picky and didn't want to try new things
because I was so used to eating so much dense food. When I
got to middle school I began to be homeschooled and that

proved only to be much worse for my diet. Food was available to me all throughout the day and that's when I believe my bad relationship with food really started. By the time I reached the 8th grade I was 175lbs and was really embarrassed. My dad (who I visited mainly in the summers) is a runner and I told him that I wanted to be able to run with him so he started training me with walking/running helping me work my way up to running the whole distance. That summer I lost 10lbs and I was stoked about it! However, I left knowing it would be difficult to do it on my own back home. I didn't have a great place to work out and my mom didn't want me going out alone so I only focused on my diet. I cut out sweets and soda for 30 days at a time with 1 day in between and by Christmas that year I'd lost another 10lbs! Over the next year or so I lost a total of about 40lbs and have maintained it still to this day. However, my relationship with food is still something I struggle with. My weight over the past few years has fluctuated within 15lbs or so due to binge eating. I'll go through seasons where I'll eat well and workout and lose a few pounds and then other times when I'll pig out. What has helped me is being honest with a few trusted people about where I'm at so that I can move forward and pinpoint the times and places I struggle the most so that I can take steps to improve. I eat a plant-based diet and my goal is for it to be completely whole foods, not processed. Currently, I'm focusing on trying to incorporate more and more of the good stuff so as to leave little room for the bad stuff. I have changed significantly over the years and am so grateful for it but I hope to continue to heal my unhealthy relationship with food as time goes on."[3]

Recap

As you can see, an eating disorder is possible for anyone. It does not matter what stage of life you are in or how strong your relationship with Jesus is. In fact, each one of these girls had a relationship with Jesus (whether deep or surface level) before going through their struggles. This brings me to one point I want to make- trials are still real and still true for each and everyone of us. In fact in James 1:1-3, Jesus says,

" Count it all joy, my brothers, when you meet trials of various kinds, for you know that the testing of your faith produces steadfastness."

Jesus specifically tells each and every one of us in this verse that we ARE going to face trials. Trials and hardships are inevitable if you follow Jesus, because through the trial is where you produce faith and full-reliance in Jesus. You see, in order for each of those girls to come up out of their circumstances and have joy and peace in the life they were given, they had to surrender everything to God and have faith that He would resurrect them from their struggles. Which brings me to this- life without Jesus is impossible and simply cannot be lived.

When we become selfish and seek the desires of our heart, rather than the will God has for us, we allow ourselves to fall into a trap the enemy has lined up for us. In other words, pursuing a "perfect" body and a "perfect" relationship with food over a relationship with Jesus, will leave you more broken and more desperate than you were before. This is why I believe so many young women are falling down this path of brokenness. We're trying to pursue "perfect" when there is no perfect with Jesus. The only thing that can be perfect IS Jesus.

In fact, I personally believe none of us have a perfect relationship with food or the way we view our bodies. I believe all of us have some sort of unhealthy relationship or mindset towards food, exercise, and/or our bodies. Since none of us are perfect, we have our faults. I guarantee that every women has looked at their body at least once and thought negatively about it. Maybe for you it's,

"I wish I had bigger boobs"
"I wish my stomach was flatter"
"I wish I didn't have such wide hips."
"Why do I have to be so skinny?"
"I wish my hair was a different color."
"I wish my butt was as big as hers."

Talking negatively to ourselves comes in many different forms, but no matter what the form, we are all guilty of it. Why? Because we were born imperfect and no matter what, will always be imperfect.

So I know what you're thinking, "Okay so I'm imperfect and I think negatively about myself, but how do I turn that around so I can have a healthy relationship with this area of my life?" Well, it begins with understanding a few truths about yourself, then cultivating a few ideas into your life…

Cultivating Truth .... Chapter 4

"So whether we are here in this body or away from this body, our goal is to please him."

2 Corinthians 5:9

Beauty From Within

"Don't be concerned about the outward beauty of fancy hairstyles, expensive jewelry, or beautiful clothes. You should clothe yourselves instead with the beauty that comes from within, the unfading beauty of a gentle and quiet spirit, which is so precious to God." -1 Peter 3:3-4

When looking at our beauty, it is important to first, look at the beauty within us- the beauty of our heart. 1 Peter Chapter 3 also says, God looks at our heart and *delights* in it. He delights in our heart when we pursue its gentle, gracious nature. Ultimately, The Lord cares much more about our heart, then our outward experience. The Lord doesn't care whether you have that new Tory Burch purse or those new Nike tennis shoes. He doesn't even care if you have tummy rolls or a six pack. He pays **no** attention to your physical appearance. LADIES- is this not the most comforting to know? We have a loving God who is after our hearts, our attention, and our love for him.

So how do you have a beautiful heart? Having a beautiful heart starts with having a relationship with Jesus, who has the *ultimate beautiful heart!* It starts with falling in love with Jesus, more than yourself, more than your physical and emotional desires. Jesus is the center of everything in your heart- the center of your relationships, your health, your image- EVERYTHING. Once Jesus is the center of everything, the desires of your heart will align with Jesus. Your heart will become gracious and gentle. Your heart will overflow with love, compassion, and sympathy.

Then, naturally, the beauty from within, will not just stay inward, but overflow into your outward beauty. Naturally, you develop a gracious and gentle attitude towards your body. The overflow of love affects how you feel about your image and your health. You develop love, compassion, and sympathy for your body.

Cultivating a beautiful heart turns your innermost desires from being you-focused to becoming Jesus-focused.

Purpose

Through cultivating Jesus into your heart and into your life, you find your purpose- Jesus reveals His purpose for your life. Because here's the truth: you were designed by God, on purpose, for a purpose, and with a purpose.

"For we are God's workmanship, created in Christ Jesus to do good works, which God prepared in advance as our way of life." -Ephesians 2:10

Not only did God create you, but He created you with intention. He created you with a specific purpose to fulfill on this earth.

Let me tell you what your purpose is *not*. Your purpose is not to be defined by food- an overconsumption or an underconsumption of food. Your purpose is not to be overly obsessed in living a healthy lifestyle that leaves your life full of guilt and regret every time you stumble. Your purpose is not to live under strict diet regimens and exercise routines. Your purpose is not to obsess with your body and your image. Your purpose is not to become too concerned with yourself, that you forget about what all God has to offer you. You see, when you trap yourself in this restrictive lifestyle, you miss out on three things:

1) Community

Picture this: your friend asks you out to dinner this weekend. "Where?" you ask. She responds with a restaurant you're not comfortable going to eat at. You say you're busy for the weekend to prevent going out to dinner and being faced with eating a meal you don't agree with. Or maybe you turn down a weekend trip with your friends because you fear there won't be healthy meals for you to eat there or you fear you won't have a place to workout. The thought of leaving your kitchen terrifies you. The thought of not being able to make your food terrifies you. Before you know it, you've isolated yourself from community, because you would rather stay in the comfort of your own house and your own kitchen, than sacrifice eating something "bad" for your body.

I know this, because this is how I used to feel and let me tell you, it didn't feel great. This is not God's best for you. He wants you to be able to experience the community he has provided for you. You weren't made to do life alone. You were made for community because in community there is LIFE. In community you can have an abundance of joy, greater than any amount of joy you can find in food.

Once I found myself surrendering my eating habits to the Lord, I was able to find freedom in all the community that he had for me. I was finally able to go out to a restaurant with my friends and order a piece of cake with them. I encourage you to do the same. Surrender your feelings and your desires for living a life full of "perfect" foods and "perfect" meals. Once you hand this over to Jesus, you can engage in the fruit He has for you!

2) Hearing from Jesus

Living a life where having a perfect body is your main desire, you miss out on the desires that Jesus has for you. Look at it this way- you can't worship two things at once. You either worship Jesus or you worship a perfect body image. When you choose to worship a perfect body image, all of your time and energy goes into this. This becomes your main priority, your main desire, and your main focus. Choosing this fleshly desire over Jesus, sets the enemy up to consume your life with it. Pursuing this body consumes your thoughts. Every action you make, revolves around this one desire to be "fit," "skinny," or "healthy." In other words, a perfect lifestyle becomes an idol that you choose to worship over God. You make no time for The Lord and His words, but rather always make time for a healthy lifestyle. Until you let Him reign sovereign over your life, you'll never hear what He has to say to you. So break down these walls. Listen to the desires of His heart over the desires of yours.

3) Joy

Jesus wants you to live a life full of *joy* and *freedom*. BUT here's the catch- joy can only be found in HIM. Joy cannot be found in the things of this world- food, the gym, a perfect body, the perfect hair, the perfect skin… Trying to find joy in your fleshly desires will leave you feeling hopeless. You'll be left searching for more and more, until you feel satisfied. Let me let you in on a little secret- you will never find eternal satisfaction and joy in the things on this earth. Eternal joy is found only in the creator of it ALL.

Every morning, you have to wake up and choose to follow Him. You have to make the decision to pursue Him over everything you may desire in this world. You must choose to seek joy in HIM. Once you choose joy in Jesus, you will finally be able to experience true and *everlasting joy*.

Overall, we each have a gift given by God that we need to use to fulfill his purpose for our lives. Take a minute right now to ask God was His purpose is for your life and to reveal to you the gift He has equipped you with to pursue His calling on your life.

Your body is a Temple

"Don't you realize that your body is the temple of the Holy Spirit, who lives in you and was given to you by God? You do not belong to yourself, for God bought you with a high price. So you must honor God with your body." -1 Corinthians 6:15-20

As followers of Christ, we must realize that our bodies are not our own, but rather are God's. Jesus purchased us with his blood and sacrifice. He died a cruel death for us, so that we may have the privilege to live on this earth. Therefore, as a temple of Jesus Christ, we must honor Him and ultimately *praise* Him for everything He has done for us.

Jesus didn't have to suffer for you and me. In fact, He could have left us to suffer on our own, but He didn't. He saw potential and a future in every single one of us. He saw a future of believers pursuing God's calling and will for their lives. So let's step into a life full of complete praise and honor for the one who reigns, the one with ultimate authority over ALL.

What exactly does that look like for each of us? Well, when we begin to honor God with our lives, we will begin to see a difference in the way we eat, the way we exercise, and the thoughts we have towards our bodies. Once we surrender our bodies to Jesus, our thoughts will go from "I wish I had her body" to "I love my body the way God has designed it to be."

From "I need to exercise because I just ate that cake" to "I need to exercise for my body and my overall health so that I can move and pursue God's calling," and even from obsessing over calorie counting and tracking how many calories you burn, to deleting the calorie tracker app and exercising without focusing on calories burned.

Eating turns into something you intentionally do for hunger and nourishment. Exercise turns into a way for you to grow your muscles, reduce risk for disease, and increase your endurance.

You see, if we could realize the plan set out for our lives and the truths that God believes about us, then we could finally step into a life of *full* wellness. Everything we invested into our bodies and our health would be for the ultimate goal of being able to pursue God even more focused than we could before. Pursuing a healthy lifestyle means we can pursue God better. If we're healthy physically and mentally, then we can get out there and reach God's people whole-heartedly. Ultimately, pouring into other's cups requires a filled cup, which starts with you. So my question is, are you filling your cup up? Are you looking to Jesus for fulfillment first, then allowing him to give you the correct desires for health?

The Healthiest You .... Chapter 5

"So whether you eat or drink, or whatever you do, do it all for the glory of God."

1 Corinthians 10:31

Myths that Took Over My Life

"I can't eat this because I read an article the other day that said it would make me fat." Many fall victim of this statement, including me. Google can be dangerous. Pinterest can be dangerous. It was through these networks that I started to believe these 10 myths listed below:

1. I can't eat bread because it makes me fat and bloated.
2. I can't eat rice because it's a carb.
3. I need to limit my carb intake if I want to be skinny.
4. No more chocolate
5. Dairy will make me fat. No dairy.
6. If it's low in calories than I can eat it and won't get fat.
7. As long as it's healthy, I can eat as much as I want.
8. I need to eat a ton of protein and few carbohydrates if I want to lose fat and gain muscle.
9. All processed food is bad for my body.

Making healthy food choices can be tough, let me tell you. The world likes to tell us what foods we shouldn't eat, what the best diet is, what foods make us fat, etc. I honestly believe that if we listened to every article on the web, our day-to-day diet would consist of nothing. Absolutely nothing.

A Well-Rounded Diet

So instead of spending every waking moment of your life on Pinterest searching "paleo meals" or "foods to make me skinny," look to the *USDA My Plate* requirements, which ensures a healthy eating lifestyle through five main food groups: fruits, vegetables, grains, protein, and dairy. Below is listed the requirements for an active teenage girl who is looking to maintain weight:

FRUITS:

- Serving size: 2 cups per day[1]
- For example, 1 small apple, 1 banana, a cup of fruit juice, or ½ cup dried fruit.

It is important that your fruit servings are majority whole fruits, over juices. This helps you to limit the sugar-intake and benefit from the dietary fiber whole fruit provides![2] If you struggle with getting your fruit servings in, here are a few ways I enjoy fruit: topping my oatmeal with slices bananas or warmed berries, drinking a fruit smoothie as a snack, topping yogurt with berries, dipping sliced apples into nut butter, and even adding berries to a summer salad!

VEGETABLES

- Serving size: 2 ½ cups per day[3]
- For example, 1 small baked sweet potato, a cup of broccoli, or 2 cups of leafy greens.

To avoid adding unnecessary sugars into your diet, choose all-natural sauces made without sugar. Choose fresh vegetables over packaged vegetables with added butter or salt for flavor. When buying canned vegetables (beets, beans, corn, etc.), look for all-natural products to avoid any added sugars, sodium, or chemicals[4]. Lastly, have fun with your veggies! Enjoy carrots and celery sticks with hummus, have a salad with dinner, cook up a roasted veggie bowl for dinner (as seen in the recipe portion). Whatever you do, don't stick with the same old veggies! Make your diet colorful!

GRAINS

- Serving Size: 6 ounces per day[5]
- For example, 1 slice of bread, ½ cup cooked oatmeal/rice/pasta, and 3 cups of popcorn.

With grains, it is important that you choose whole grains over refined grains[6]. The American diet is full of hamburger buns, processed cereals, donuts, and every other glutinous product you can think of! Unfortunately, many don't think about the value of the grains their eating. To give your body the good fiber and carbohydrates it needs, without the processed ingredients, substitute a white bread with whole grain bread! Also, an easy way to tell if your bread is full of processed sugars and chemicals is with this technique: smoosh a slice of bread in your hand. If it stays rolled into a ball the size of your fist, then throw it away! If it unravels or crumbles into pieces, eat it!

Easy ways to incorporate nutritional WHOLE grains into your diet can be: eating ½ cup of cooked oatmeal or 2 slices of whole grain toast spread with peanut butter and banana for breakfast, brown rice or quinoa as a side for lunch or dinner, or even popcorn as an afternoon snack (not the movie-theater kind people, choose natural popcorn!)

PROTEIN

- Serving Size: 5 ½ ounces per day[7]
- For example, 1 egg, 1 tbsp nut butter, 2 tbsp hummus, or 1 ounce of lean meat.

What's best to remember when incorporating protein, is to include a *variety* of choices! If you're a meat-eater, there are many options for protein: beef, chicken, salmon, the list goes on! It's also important to remember to eat more lean protein, than fatty protein- beef, bacon, bologna, etc[8]. More lean meat choices include chicken breast, turkey, ham, and much more! Fish is always a good idea too since most fish is FULL of omega-3 fatty acids aka the *good* fats! My favorites to eat are chicken, salmon, and tuna!

For vegetarians, ways to incorporate protein can be through eggs in any form, beans, nut products, or tofu!

DAIRY

- Serving Size: 3 cups a day[9]
- For example, 1 cup of milk, 1 cup of yogurt, or ⅓ cup of shredded cheese.

When choosing dairy, choose low-fat or non-fat more than whole[10]. For example, choose non-fat yogurt, low-fat cheese, or non-fat milk. If you have trouble incorporating dairy into your daily routine, try making your oatmeal with milk, eating yogurt with fruit and granola for breakfast, blend yogurt and/or milk with fruit to make a smoothie... Looking for a new beverage? Drink a glass of milk! If you're lactose intolerant or follow a vegan diet, don't worry! There's ways for you to get your calcium too! You can find calcium in almond milk-based yogurts, milks, and even cheeses! For me, I enjoy nonfat yogurt (my favorite is Siggis!) as a breakfast meal, snack, and sometimes even dessert! For milk, I absolutely love drinking almond milk! I add it to my oats, baked goods, and even my coffee! Oh! That reminds me! Next time you go to Starbucks or Dunkin Donuts or whatever hole-in-the-wall coffee shop you enjoy (because let's be honest, they always have the best coffee), choose nonfat milk, almond milk, or even coconut milk for your lattes! Better yet- ditch the high-sugar lattes all-together!

Well, of course enjoy one every once in awhile! Balance people!

Finding the Perfect Balance of Calories

So now that you know what foods your "diet" should consist of to ensure you are getting all of the proper nutrients you need to grow, it's time to look at what a healthy amount of calories that translates too. Finding the "perfect" balance of calories for your "diet" can be hard, confusing, but also very important. We all need to find that perfect balance of calories, to make sure we are not overfeeding or underfeeding ourselves, day-to-day.

Consuming too few calories slows down your metabolism, causing you to save all the energy you have and therefore, not burn calories[11]. And because of the lack of protein, your body goes to your muscles for energy. As a result, you'll begin to lose muscle and keep all the fat you're trying so desperately to lose[11]. In the end, too few calories causes your body to go into starvation mode, holding onto all the fat/energy you have already to make sure your body is getting what it needs to survive. Isn't it crazy how our bodies have a way of doing everything it possibly can to keep us alive?

Along with a decreased metabolism, the body also experiences a hormonal imbalance. The stress that the body is put under from starvation and the lack of body fat can lower the hormonal levels of estrogen, a vital hormone for reproduction, in your body[12]. The body either stops producing or produces very little of estrogen. As a result, your menstruation cycle, as talked about earlier, can become irregular and even completely disappear[13].

On the other hand, consuming too many calories can also put a strain on your body! I'm not talking about the days you decide to treat yourself. No, definitely not. I'm talking about overindulging every day. An overconsumption of your dietary needs results in weight gain and many other side-effects, as talked about earlier!

So, what IS the perfect balance of calories, you're wondering? Well, medically speaking, as active teenage girls, we should be consuming anywhere from 1,800 to 2,200 calories per day to maintain a healthy weight[14]! Many girls believe they need to be consuming around 1,200 to 1,500 because maybe that's what they heard from their mother or from a source online. The problem with those numbers is they're not realistic, at all. Did you know our bodies naturally burn that SAME range of calories day-to-day, EVEN on your lazy days. Shocking, I know. Those numbers also don't take into account physical activity and the amount of calories you burn from it! Not only that, but those restrictive numbers completely miss the fact that as a teenage girl, you are still growing. In order to grow, have a regular period, and be active, you *need* the correct amount of fuel! Food is the fuel!

Although it is important to be knowledgeable about how many calories your body needs to maintain its weight AND fuel your day-to-day activities, it is also very important to realize that balancing your calories shouldn't be something you obsess over. My goal in telling you how many calories we need as active women, is so that you may understand your body needs a lot more than you think it does. We weren't meant to live on 1,200 calories diets. So if you're one of those girls trying to live on a low-calorie diet, set yourself free! Give your body the fuel it needs and so desperately wants from you! In fact, if you only get one thing out of this, let it be this- STOP COUNTING YOUR CALORIES. Delete your calorie tracker app. Delete the option to track how many calories you've burned on your activity tracker. Delete it all. It's time we look at food as fuel for our bodies, rather than something we can count. This is life, not math class.

Where Should My Calories Come From?

Well, to answer that short and quick, your calories should be 50 percent **carbohydrates**, 30 percent **fat** and 20 percent **protein**[15]!

Contrary to popular belief, your body *needs* carbs to survive. The media portrays carbs negatively, encouraging us to cut out all carbs from our diets. Maybe you've looked at a tabloid article or a picture on Pinterest and been completely convinced that you need to cut out all pasta, bagels, and bread from your diet because they're the enemy and the source of all fat. Okay, first off, no. That is not true one bit. Unfortunately, what many people don't realize is carbohydrates are actually our body's *first* and *main* source of energy[16]. Which means? You need carbs the MOST! Carbohydrates replenish your muscle glycogen after you exercise and work your muscles[17]!

I am sure we have all heard runners talk about the big bowl of pasta they ate the night before a big run. We all know sports players are always told to load up on carbs before a game. But guess what? If you're going to hit the gym to lift some weights, your body needs the carb load-up too! Whether you're lifting weights or going on a run, your body needs carbs. The carbs we consume are stored in your muscles, ready for to fuel those muscles when you work em! Of course, you also need protein. Protein is a good source of calories to consume after a workout, along with carbohydrates, because of its ability to protect, repair, and build your muscles[17]!

Now, we can't forget about fats! When I say fats, I mean the healthy fats. Healthy fats can be found in avocados, ghee butter, nut butters, and oils. In moderation, these fats are NOT bad for you. Of course their name makes you think differently, but fats are actually another important nutrient our bodies need for proper digestion[16]! There are two types of fats we need- saturated (solid) and unsaturated (liquid) and one type of fat we don't need- trans. Trans fats is an artificial fat. Getting the right amount of fats helps us to absorb vitamins and antioxidants.

To have a well rounded diet we need a proper amount of carbohydrates, proteins, and fats in our meals. Carbohydrates provide us with the energy we need, proteins slow down digestion, and fats allow our bodies to absorb the nutrients it needs.

Snacking

Okay I know I'm not the only one who gets hungry between lunch and dinner… it's pretty much inevitable. This is why afternoon snacks are a thing for me. I know that if I didn't have my afternoon snack, then I would be a hangry monster by the time dinner rolled around. IN fact, I know this all too well from the days of restrictive eating. As I eluded to earlier, I had a strict eating schedule I forced myself to follow. Breakfast. Lunch. Dinner. 4 hours between each meal. 300 to 400 calories for each meal. I never allowed myself to snack, no matter how hungry I was because of the horrible connotation I had made with it, due to all of the inaccurate information I read on the Internet.

If you didn't already know, there's a huge debate on whether snacking between meals is "good" or "bad" for your body and if it will make you lose or gain weight. Every day you can find a new article or blog to post about it, trying to tell YOU what is good for YOUR body. And I am going to be the first to say, don't listen. Put down your phone and listen to your body. You know your body better than the person who posted that blog. Only you can understand what your body truly needs. Our bodies each have a unique ways of metabolizing foods. The amount and rate of digestion can vary greatly from person to person.. That being said, there is no way one guideline can fit every single one of our bodies. So do what fits YOU.

Some days, you'll be more hungry than others. Some days you'll eat tons of food and never feel full and other days you may only need 3 meals. Each day is different, full of different foods, different circumstances, and different amounts of activity. This is why no flat amount of calories, meals, or snacks can be set. The new guideline that needs to be set is this- eat when your body is telling you to eat. Eat when your stomach grumbles. Eat when you *need* food. Stop eating when you're full. Don't eat a meal just for the sake of it. Eat for fuel.

Why listening to your body and eating a snack is smart...

We ask a lot from our bodies., They burn a lot of energy throughout the day. Just think for a second about everything you do in a day, every task you accomplish, every activity you engage in, every bit of homework you complete… Our bodies are always working, whether at school, a job, in a sport, and even at home! It would only make sense that we fuel our body with those tasks in mind! This is why snacking is so important. A nutritious snack can rid your hunger, so you can finally focus on getting work done. With a full tummy, you'll be able to focus in class or that long dreadful meeting… Besides that obvious benefit, a snack also has the benefit of giving you the brain-power to conquer exam week. OR that pile of homework you set aside, as you picked up this book (caught ya). Later I'll be expanding a little more on snacking, and it's wonderful capability of turning a crummy workout into a GREAT workout.

Food does a lot more than we give it credit for. For so long, I looked at food as an enemy to avoid as much as possible, rather than a friend that we ALL literally need to survive! Make friends with food, because after all, it's here to stay and you'll ALWAYS need it.

What makes a good snack + what snacks should look like

A healthy and nutritious snack should be full of carbohydrates, fiber, and a little bit of protein to hold you over until dinner[18]. Before having a snack, check the ingredients label. Avoid snacks that are high in added sugar, fat, or artificial ingredients[19]. Try to choose whole foods over drinks- the nutritional value is greater and will fill you up longer. Also try to choose snacks as close as possible to their whole form[19]. For example, choose an apple over apple juice or maybe a baked potato over potato chips. Whole grains make the best snacks because they're full of carbohydrates and fiber and have a moderate amount of calories[19]. Below are a few examples of healthy snacks full of carbohydrates, fiber, and protein.

- Hard boiled egg with 1 cup carrots
- 1 tbsp peanut butter with apple or banana
- 1 container of yogurt (I prefer Siggi's because it is all natural and has low sugar) with berries
- 2 tbsp hummus with 1 cup celery and 1 cup carrots
- 1 cup pistachios
- 1/4 cup mixed nuts

- 1 slice of whole grain toast with 1 tbsp peanut butter
- 1 low-fat cheese stick with either 1 cup veggies of choice or with an apple

With these healthy snack tips and choices, you'll feel full, energized, and ready to put your brain to any task ahead. And remember, snacking is always a good idea when it looks THIS good.

Overall, there are many tips and tricks to healthy eating that you and I can follow to ensure a healthy lifestyle. Each of our bodies have a certain amount of calories we need in order to to maintain a healthy body at a healthy weight. These calories should come from the right amount of carbohydrates, fats, and proteins which we get from five food groups. These five food groups should be included in each and every one of our diets. Fruits, vegetables, grains, protein, and dairy are an important part of a healthy lifestyle.. The way we incorporate these different groups of foods into our diets is going to look different to each and every one of us. Our bodies were designed differently and desire different things. It's important to remember that the road to a perfect diet begins with a variety of whole, colorful foods!

How eating healthy affects you physically

As you begin to incorporate these new healthy tips and tricks into your life, you will see a corresponding change on your body physically and mentally. You will see obvious changes in your overall appearance. Your body shape may change. Your skin may change, becoming clear and smooth! Your hair may even change! Because when you give your body the proper nutrients it needs, your hair, skin, and nails are given what they need to grow and become strong. Your bodies will now begin to function how they were designed to. Every organ and working system in your body will be able to perform at its best. Giving your body the proper nutrients it needs creates a happy digestive system and immune system allowing them to function and function *well.*

How eating healthy affects you mentally

What you put into your body also has the ability to affect your mood, your attitude, and your emotions. The naturally occurring chemicals in foods affect your brain and its ability to function correctly. Real, whole foods can leave you feeling happy and full of energy. Other processed foods can leave you feeling run down, cranky, or hormonal. How much you eat also has the ability to affect your brain and your mood status. Just to recap, eating too few nutrients can leave you feeling sad, alone, stressed, or anxious. But when you give your body the proper amount of nutrients and calories it needs, your mood will change to bright and your outlook will become positive!

The food we consume day-to-day has the ability to affect so much more than we give it credit.

The Active You .... Chapter 6

"I plead with you to give your bodies to God because of all He has done for you. Let them be a living and holy sacrifice... This is truly the way to worship Him."

Romans 12:1

My Old Exercise Pattern

Exercise for me has never been something I considered as a way to take care of my body, but rather as way for me to punish my body. Exercise has always been something I've hated, pretty much completely dreaded.

Growing up, I was *never* athletic. I played upward soccer for one year as a little munchkin, then never again. Not exactly sure why, but it probably had to do with the fact that I didn't score one goal the whole year and would have rather sat on the ball and have pictures taken of me, than run around the field chasing that very ball.

Later, I tried upward basketball, to which I made one basket the whole season, during the last game of the season. Clearly I wasn't good at that sport either. Then, in middle school, I tried volleyball. My mom and all of my sisters played volleyball, so this was a sport I desperately wanted to excel in, but unfortunately, did not. I failed to make the team in eighth grade, then stopped trying from there.

"I guess I'm just not made out to play a sport like all my friends and family. I'm just not good enough," These were the thoughts I started to have consistently. I remember feeling embarrassed, not good enough, and left out. All my friends were playing a sport and I wasn't. They were all connecting through volleyball and meanwhile, I was sitting in the stands wishing to be included.

Through all of those years, I never looked at sports as a way to get out there and move my body. Sports were a way for me to feel included, be involved, and socialize. That all changed freshmen year of high school.

Freshmen year, my friend and I decided to condition with the lacrosse team for the fall/winter months. Neither of us were active, so we saw this as a way to "get in shape."

Surprisingly, by the end of the winter months, we agreed to join the lacrosse team. Finally- a sport I fell in love with and felt like I could excel in!

I stuck with lacrosse for two-ish years- through evil coaches, health issues, and all. I played varsity during the school year and enjoyed club over the summer. I felt like I was finally succeeding in a sport I loved! Then junior year hit. ANOTHER new coach came in. In my eyes, he was a complete jerk and quickly turning the team into a bunch of cliquey, preppy girls. I walked away from lacrosse that year. This was also a way for me to finally set myself free from Woodmont (the school I switched from, as you learned earlier).

In attempts to stay active, I joined the soccer team for my own school (they needed players and my friend convinced me to join). Guys. I sat the bench 90% of the season. It was horrible. And looking back on it now, I really only joined for the social aspect and the opportunity to hang out with a boy I liked. UGHHHHH. (Yes, I played a sport I absolutely hated, just to impress a stupid senior boy, who only wanted me for his pleasure. It's amazing what girls will do for immature high school boys, isn't it?)

So, as you're probably wondering, where did I go from there? Yeah, you guessed it, I quit sports for the rest of my life. And you know what I realized, I wasn't made out for sports, but that's okay. God creates us all differently, with different skills, and different desires.

In NEW attempts to stay active, I ran, like everyday. This was my new "sport." I liked this sport. It was by myself, no one to compete with, and no one to impress- just me and the road. Also, it was free, required no hand-eye (or foot-eye?) coordination, and could be done whenever I felt like it. And there lies the issue... I ran whenever I felt like it. Which means, I ran whenever I felt the guilt, shame, and regret of my body and my eating choices. And here is where I repeat-

Exercise for me has never been something I considered a way to take care of my body, but rather as way for me to punish my body.

Myths About Exercise

Just as with my eating habits, I developed myths about exercise.The whole year before I realized I was deep in an unhealthy lifestyle, exercise was only ever a compensatory behavior to me. If I felt fat, I went on a run. If I looked in the mirror and didn't like what I saw, I did crunches. If I ate a piece of cake and immediately regretted it, I would do jumping jacks in the kitchen. Honestly, it became obsessive, as you can see. To illustrate how it turned into a form of punishment for me, here are the myths I developed towards exercise...

1. If I do crunches and planks every day, I'll get abs.
2. Doing jumping jacks after I ate that cake with erase all the calories.
3. The only way to lose weight is to run every day.
4. Screw strength training, that's for boys.
5. If I just run every day, I will increase my core strength.

Okay, that was pretty embarrassing to tell you and I feel silly even writing those things, but maybe you've thought them too? Now maybe you don't feel so alone, as I did. Regardless of how we feel and how we think... ladies, exercise should not be looked at this way. Unfortunately, I was clueless as to what physical activity really was, how it should be incorporated into my life, and the exact benefits of incorporating it into my lifestyle. But fortunately, for you, I have learned the positive aspects of exercise and why *you* should incorporate it into your daily routine.

AHA Requirements for Exercise

According to The American Heart Association (AHA), it is recommended that you and I participate in 150 minutes of moderate exercise or 75 minutes of vigorous exercise (or a combination of moderate and vigorous exercise) per week[1]. An easy way to make this happen is by incorporating 30 minutes of moderate aerobic activity in 5 days of your week or 25 minutes of vigorous aerobic activity in 3 days of your week[1]. It is also recommended that you and I participate in moderate to high-intensity muscle-strengthening exercises for at least two days of the week[1]. Through aerobic and strength exercises, these basic recommendations help to ensure overall cardiovascular health (heart, stamina, and flexibility)[1].

So, what are different ways to make sure you are getting in these daily minutes of exercise? Look below to find out!

Types of Exercise

Just in case you didn't know, physical activity is *anything* that gets your body up and moving. Whaaat, forreal?! Yes! Exercise doesn't have to be as scary as you make it out to be ladies! In fact, I guarantee you exercise is something we are all capable of, but there's a secret to it… According to my mentor Melissa Shotkoski, the secret to engaging in exercise and loving it at the same time, is having a variety of activities that you love[2]! In fact, AHA also recommends that we have a variety of exercises incorporated in our daily routine- aerobic (endurance), strength, and balance and stretching[1].

1)   **Aerobic exercise**, also referred to as endurance exercise[3], is the type that comes to most of our minds when we think about exercise. This is the oh-so-dreadful cardio activity you think of- aka running, the elliptical, the stair-stepper… pretty much anything that increases your breathing and heart rate. This is where the "30 minutes per day" comes in.

But wait. Let me just pause before your self doubt gets the best of you (because, girl, I know you're having those feelings right now). I am here to tell you, cardio doesn't have to be dreadful! In fact, cardio can be found in almost anything, as long as it increases your breathing and heart rate! Even things you may love!

A few moderate-intensity examples that may catch your eye (and your satisfaction) a little better[4]…

- Walking
- Tennis doubles
- A light bike ride
- Golf
- Volleyball
- Canoeing/kayaking
- Gymnastics
- Slow dancing

And then, a few vigorous-intensity examples of exercise that may interest you in becoming active[4]…

- Aerobic Dancing
- Swimming
- Going on a hike
- Jumping rope
- Bicycling (more than 10 mph)
- Boxing, basketball, soccer, lacrosse, etc

2)   Strength and resistance training is another form of exercise, recommended that we incorporate into at least two days of of our weekly routine[5]. Wait, really? "I thought that was just for for people who loved crossfit, people who wanted to become body-builders." Psych. Strength training is for everyone! Why? Because strength training builds stronger muscles, important for you to function in your favorite activities, protect your body from injury, and increase your overall metabolism!

I know, I know- you're still caught up in the idea of body-builders. Fortunately, strength-training isn't just lifting crazy amounts of weights. Strength training can be a variety of things, because in exercise, there is ALWAYS variety! So, how can you strengthen your muscles? Through the use of free weights, machines, and even your own body[5]! That's right, you heard me! You don't even need a gym full of weights and machines to build strong muscles. Your body is the perfect, free access gateway to strong muscles!

My recommendation for you is to split your training up into muscle groups. For example, one day you work on arms, another day you work on legs, and a third day, you work on abs! By splitting it up, you give each muscle group the rest it needs AND you can go all out in the designated muscle group for that day! I also recommend that you find a good workout program that already has the workouts set and planned. This way you can ensure you're increasing your strength and muscle mass, but also not going overboard!

Once you follow those two recs, I guarantee you'll end up falling in love with strength training, more than you would have ever though!

3)   **Balance and flexibility exercises**, I have decided to group together due to their complementing characteristics. Balance and flexibility are exercises that not many of us think of as, well, exercise! In fact, not many of us even know about it or even think about, when we think exercise. But guess what? We *all* need good balance and flexibility to be able to do the things we do everyday[6]. Flexibility also helps to widen your range of movement and lower your risk for injury, when exercising[7].

Balance can be incorporated in your everyday routine or even just a few days a week, with a few simple balancing exercises or through a yoga or tai chi class! Flexibility, on the other hand, should be incorporated into every aerobic and strength exercise routine[7]! It's best to stretch after you have already worked out since your muscles are warm and can be stretched without tightening a muscle, locking a joint, or creating unwanted pain[7]! To ensure the best outcome, go into each stretch slowly and smoothly and hold the position for 10-30 seconds[7]. Repeat each position at least 3 times! As you're going through each stretch, remember to breathe slowly, transition smoothly, and keep your joints slightly bent[7]! By following all of these guidelines, you are ensuring a safe stretch, preventing injury!

Other easy ways to incorporate a good stretch sesh into your routine, can be through a yoga class or pilates class! If you choose to sign up for one of those though, it's always good to drink tons of water before AND after, to replenish all the muscles you just stretched. (A lack of water consumption afterwards can create cramping in stretched areas.)

There are SO many ways for you to get your body moving! You don't have to be young and fit to exercise nor do you need an excuse to exercise. We are ALL capable of moving our bodies! After addressing the different forms of exercise and different ways to get involved in each, I hope exercise isn't as scary and intimidating as you once thought it to be, because I guarantee it's not. I can say that because I used to be there, terrified of exercise. I was always scared of incorporating new forms of activity, other than running, into my routine because I felt unequipped and weak. I was too afraid to dive into new exercise routines because failure was always in the back of my mind. Failure was my default (from the seemingly endless amount of sports I failed at), so naturally, I assumed I would fail at anything other than running. In fact, I absolutely refused to get involved in strength training because of its connotation to heavy weights and hard machines.

Not only was my default mindset failure, but my knowledge of different exercise routines was lacking. Going back to the five myths I told you before, this is where they played in. Because I knew nothing about exercise and was relying on Pinterest workouts and tabloids to direct my exercise routine, I developed my own ideas about exercise, all of which were very very wrong.

As you have just read, exercise does in fact, have a definition and an exact purpose in the daily routine of each and every one of our lives. Along with defining exercise and its purpose, I also want to share with you all a few benefits exercise can provide you with!

Benefits of Exercise-Physical

So when talking about the benefits of exercise, I know your mind immediately focuses on those body transitions that ALL of us want: a six pack, skinny legs, muscular-toned arms... Because that's what most people think about when they think exercise isn't it? Unfortunately, that's also what immediately comes to my mind. Even today, if someone were to ask me, "What does being physically fit look like to you?" I would honestly answer with that exact list, or something similar. Whether you agree or not, this is all a result of our culture and what our society portrays as "health."

When people are looking to get involved in an exercise program, the main reasons for doing so are for the physical outcomes. Don't get me wrong, that's great motivation! I believe being physically fit and tone and in-shape is wonderful! BUT I do believe that should not be the only focus of exercise, because then it turns into a forced activity, something that we do just for an image. And as I will explain later, exercise should be WAY more than that.

So, looking past the toned tummy we all secretly want deep down, why should you and I exercise? The answer to that is this, for our overall physical health- our internal organs and organ systems! As you begin to move your body the way that it was designed to move, you decrease your risk for developing a cardiovascular disease[8]. Not only will you be at a lower risk for developing a heart disease, but also be at a stable level of blood pressure and good cholestero[8]l. I know you may be thinking these are things you don't need to worry about, but just think with me for a second. As you get older, do you want to be faced with heart disease or diabetes? If your answer was no, then you SHOULD be worrying about those things because in the end, heart problems and diabetes is what you could end up with!

Not only can it prevent serious concerns as listed above, but less serious problems too!
Moving your body every day for at least thirty minutes can:

- Maintain your weight
- Prevent bone loss
- Boost your energy
- Improve sleep patterns
- Increases muscle strength
- Improves your endurance
- Maintains quality of life [8]

Along with the physical effects exercise has on our bodies, it can also have positive mental effects. This isn't necessarily common knowledge, which is why I believe exercise has such a horrible connotation related to it. For those who completely deny exercising and just refuse to even go there, do you know how much being active can actually affect you mentally and emotionally?! I did NOT. As I told you earlier, I've always looked at exercise through the eyes of sports, and never outside that lense. Consequently, I was never able to see the affects exercise had on me emotionally, because I was pretty much never interested in that aspect of physical activity. I was never really interested at all, to say the least.

Now that I have incorporated a solid exercise routine into my life, I am able to recognize and appreciate the true benefits that exercise can have on our mental status. Therefore, in addition to the physical affects, exercise also has the ability to improve your overall mental health [8]. Exercise releases endorphins- the "feel-good" hormone in your brain- when you exercise [9]. These endorphins are what make you feel happy and well after you workout. Because of the release of these endorphins into your brain, you may also be relieved of any stress, tension, anxiety, or depression [9]. In fact, many doctors today will recommend exercise as a way of treatment for depression[10]. Exercising daily can also improve the way you feel about your self-image and help to rid negative thoughts towards your body[10].

With benefits like these, it's amazing more people don't try incorporating exercise into their daily routines. In fact, if you are struggling with stress and anxiety from your current circumstances, I encourage you to incorporate exercise slowly into your routine.

Ultimately, everything you do in your life now will have a direct effect on the results of your life 20 years from now. So get out and move babe! Do what you love! Hike, bike, swim, skateboard, walk, the possibilities are ENDLESS. Exercise doesn't have to be long and painful. Remember! Exercise is anything that moves your body and gets your heart rate up! OH and we can't forget... gets you doing something you love!

Why you should give your body rest

Rest is something that I've had a real hard time coming to terms with and you may have too. Living in a culture that demands so many things of us, rest feels almost impossible. We're expected to get an education, get a job, have a family, spend time with friends, and oh yeah, keep up with our health. We try and try to live up to these standards, pushing our bodies to the max, past the max if we're being honest. We become lifeless people, never taking time for ourselves to fully recoup and recharge. Rest seems counterproductive to most of us. Rest may even seem like a waste of time and resources to you. "Why would I rest when I have a perfect body to maintain?" You may wonder.

Well you see, rest is actually required if you want to live a healthy life, chock full of progress. Yes, required. Rest should be in *every* workout program. When we give our bodies a day to rest, we are allowing our muscles damaged during exercise to reconstruct and recover[11]. When we exercise, especially during strength training, we put a lot of stress on our muscles. After a sweaty workout, your muscles need to rest so they can recoup and recharge so you can go *all out* in the next workout! Ideally, you should be giving the muscles you just worked a good 48 hour rest period[11]. For example, if you workout your legs one day, the next day should include endurance training or strength training of a different muscle group. (An easy schedule to follow is strength training every other day and endurance/cardio exercise on the days in-between.) During the 48 hour rest period, your muscles are given time to grow and increase in strength! Neglecting to give your muscles a good rest can hinder results[12]. By never pausing and, in fact, continuing to go go go, you're affecting your overall performance level, meaning you won't be able to go all out in your next workout.

Your may also be affecting your immune system and ability to get quality sleep at night[12]! A strained immune system increase your chance of getting sick, which then restricts your ability to exercise at all! A lack of quality sleep can increase stress levels, mood levels, and unfortunately, sugar cravings[12]. (you know those afternoon munchies I'm talking about) This is why it is so important that we listen to our bodies. If you feel a cold coming on, slow down and take a break. If you feel tired and week in your workout, rest and try the next day! Listen to your body! Unfortunately, this isn't as easy as it sounds.

But why? Why do we fear rest, if rest is SO good in the first place?! We fear doing nothing because the world makes us feel like we should always be doing something. And that's where the problem lies- we're looking to the world for all the answers, rather than the one who created everything, our lives included! How bout we look there...

"On the seventh day God had finished his work of creation, so He rested from all His work. And God blessed the seventh day and declared it holy, because it was the day when He rested from all his work of creation."
-Genesis 2:2-3

As you can see, Jesus took a rest. After six days of work, He allowed his body to have rest. He could have very easily continued to push through. In fact, He didn't even need to rest. He wasn't tired or weary. BUT He chose to take a day of sabbath to show us that we NEED rest. He declared a whole day of rest for you and for me, not so that we would have an extra day to get things done, but so that we may have an extra day to take care of ourselves.

Take advantage of the day of rest that Jesus has provided you with. Do things for yourself that would empower you throughout your hectic week. Rest day is your day! Go on a walk, read a book, watch Netflix all day... do anything that makes YOU happy.

Most importantly, do not feel obligated to restrict yourself on your day of rest. Just because you are resting your body, doesn't mean you should then put to rest your eating habits too. An exercising body needs food on its on days and off days. How else are you going to fuel your next workout?

Lastly, rest DOES NOT have to be feared ladies. Love rest. Look forward to rest. Make rest your friend.

How Exercise Changed My Life

After learning about the different forms of exercise and how our bodies do, in fact, need a variety of exercise patterns, I knew it was time to change up my routine. Honestly, running every day was getting boring and tiring and painful. Yes, painful. My knees, hips, and ankles were constantly hurting because I was never giving myself a break. My body wasn't designed to be pushed this hard, every day, with no rest and no proper fuel. For my health, I needed to incorporate other exercise routines. I was giving my body all the cardio, but never any strength exercises. How did I expect to gain muscles, if I wasn't ever putting in the work?

Eventually, I incorporated strength training into my workout routine. I began resistance training 3 days a week-Monday, Wednesday, and Friday. As you can see, I give myself a day between each workout for muscle recovery. In between the strength focused days, I train for endurance. For these days, I'll go on a long walk, a run, or do a 30 minute HIIT workout! HIIT stands for High Intensity Interval Training

After the first week of this new exercise routine, I was hooked. I fell completely in love with this routine of varied exercise . After a few weeks, all of the benefits I talked about, started to become evident in my life. My mood and attitude was starting to change; I had a more positive and happy mood all the time. I was full of SO much energy throughout my day. I was even able to focus better in school and get more work done. I also saw a huge change in my sleep patterns. I went from going to sleep late at night and barely being able to wake up for school the next morning, to going to sleep before 9pm and naturally waking up before 6am.

My body was finally getting the proper exercise it needed physically and emotionally. I finally felt healthy all around. As you can see through this example of my life, there are so many benefits to incorporating exercise into your routine. Once you pick a routine that you love and fits perfectly with your schedule, you'll begin to see the benefits play out in your life like never before. Quickly, you'll fall in love with exercise and the true benefits it brings to you life..

Why and How We Fuel For exercise

Would you expect your car to run if the gas tank was empty? No. Then why are you expecting your body to run when your stomach is empty? Pause and think about that for a second...

Just like your car cannot be used at its full potential without gas in the tank, your body cannot be used at its full potential without food stored. You're body will not reach its full potential if you are not giving it the fuel it needs to *move*. Many times, we forget this. We forget that our bodies need food, not only to survive, but to give us energy to do the everyday activities that we enjoy!

Do you ever feel weak when you exercise? Dizzy? Nauseous? Like you just can't make it through the workout without passing out or even dying? Yeah, I've been there. I used to make it through the first circuit of my workout then absolutely STRUGGLE to make it through the rest of the workout. I felt weak, tired, and super nauseous. My stomach would always start grumbling a few minutes in. I knew I was hungry, but I just wanted to power through the workout so I could eat a big meal once I was finished. Sound familiar to you?

If this is how you feel, the underlying problem you may have is a lack of pre-workout fuel. If you want to be able to go all out in your workout, you MUST fuel your body with the proper nutrients it needs to give you energy. Those proper nutrients are carbohydrates and a little bit of protein[13]. It's best to fuel up within two hours of exercising with complex carbohydrates, like whole grains[14]. Why carbohydrates? Simply because they're our bodies first source of energy! The carbs you consume are stored in the muscles and during exercise, are used as fuel[13]. You don't need too much protein before a workout; too much protein can leave your body busy digesting your food, rather than delivering blood and oxygen to your muscles, as you workout[13]. You also do not need a whole ton of fat before you workout because too much fat can also leave your body in digestive mode, rather than energy mode. Both healthy fats and proteins should be avoided before a workout to ensure a happy GI (gastrointestinal) system during your workout! A lack of carbohydrates OR too much food before a workout, can leave you feeling sluggish, nauseous, and sick to your stomach[14]. Which is never how you want to feel when trying to go all out in a workout.

An easy way to make sure you are fueling your workouts is by planning your workouts around your meals/snacks. For example, if you plan to workout early the next morning, eat a filling snack before you go to bed, including a good amount of carbs, fats, and protein to sustain you into the next morning. For some people, this should be enough to carry them into the next morning and through a early morning workout. For others, maybe not. If you find that you're hungry or dizzy when you wake up the next morning, it would be smart to snack on a banana before you hit the gym. This will give you the carbs you need to power through your workout!

Or maybe you enjoy working out in the afternoon... If this is you, make sure you plan your workout a good 2 hours after your lunch, to allow your lunch to settle in. Your lunch should be full of complex carbs that will give you energy for your workout.

Examples of some good pre-workout fuel (2 hours before) full of complex carbohydrates and some protein are

- A bowl of oatmeal made with lowfat milk and fruit
- A fruit smoothie made with fruit and lowfat milk
- Nonfat yogurt with fruit (optional: granola)
- Peanut butter toast/peanut butter sandwich

Examples of pre-workout fuel, within an hour (or less) before a workout are

- A rice cake with peanut butter
- A banana
- Dried fruit and nuts
- Applesauce

Contrary to what many believe, a pre-workout snack is *very* important if you want to have an effective workout. For many, it seems smart and beneficial to workout on an empty stomach because of the idea that your body will burn more fat that way. Not only is that false, but it can also hinder your results. A lack of fueling your body before a workout will only leave you fatigued halfway through and unable to work at your *full* potential. In the end, you'll end up burning less calories than if you fueled your body with the energy it needs to make it through the whole workout at 110%[13]. Therefore, a pre-workout snack is not only smart, but also very beneficial and vital for those muscle gains!

Why and How We Fuel After Exercise

Fueling after exercise is just as important as fueling your body before exercise. What you eat after extensive exercise is important for recovery and energy to keep you going. During exercise, your muscles are working very hard, depleting your blood of glucose in the process[13]. All of the carbohydrates you ate before the workout, are then used to give your muscles the energy to keep moving. During exercise you are using all of the stored carbohydrates in your muscles. Which means, after exercise, you must replenish all of the lost carbohydrates- your muscle glycogen[13].

In order to replenish your muscle glycogen and restore the energy just burned, you must consume an adequate amount of carbohydrates and protein after an extensive workout. Just as with your pre-workout fuel, your post-workout fuel should provide more carbohydrates than protein[14]. Because carbohydrates are the main source of energy, your muscles used up a lot of the carbohydrates for fuel. To fully recover your energy, muscles and tissues, and provide you with a better strength and performance level, carbohydrates are very important[13]. Within around 20 minutes of working out, you should consume foods high in carbohydrates, because that's when glycogen production is most active[14]. Foods high in carbohydrates perfect for fueling after a workout are oatmeal, a sweet potato, apples, bananas, or toast. In addition to the carbohydrates, you must also consume protein. Protein is important for repairing your muscles and tissue damage and also building your muscles[14]. Good sources of protein after a workout are greek yogurt, nonfat milk, nut butters, or even a preferred protein powder. Altogether... for an adequate post-workout fuel, you should be consuming a meal or snack high in carbohydrates and moderate in protein.

Looking for a good post-workout meal for fuel? Here are a few of my favorites...

- A fruit smoothie made with frozen fruit, kale, protein powder, almond milk, and chia seeds (I also love to top it with granola)
- A baked sweet potato topped with nonfat yogurt, nut butter, and my favorite granola

- ½ cup of oatmeal made with almond milk and topped with, banana slices, peanut butter, and chia seeds

Or maybe you had a meal before you worked out and you want more of a post-workout snack for fuel. Here are a few of my favorite post-workout snacks...

- A diced apple with 2 tbsp of peanut butter (or any other nut butter)
- A 4 ounce container of my favorite nonfat yogurt
- Tuna fish and crackers

As you can see, all of the above example have a combination of complex carbohydrates and protein. It is important to remember these key facts when working out because a lack of proper carbohydrates and protein after you workout can hinder your results. A lack in fuel can cause a lack in muscle gains or worse, loss of muscle tissue[14]. Which is why it is SO important to refuel after you exercise! Refueling provides you with the much-needed (and wanted) energy, growth, and muscle gains. Who doesn't want to grow stronger muscles??

The New Perspective .... Chapter 7

"For I can do everything through Christ who gives me strength."

Philippians 4:13

Coming at Exercise with a Negative Perspective

For many, when the thought of exercise first pops into our heads, we immediately envision a negative image. Unfortunately, this is a result of society and how they have displayed exercise to us. Exercise is seen (and portrayed) as activities that only the strongest and the fittest in our culture partake. No longer is exercise looked at as a way of discipline, responsibility, and stewardship of the body. Often we see exercise displayed as a form of punishment for our bodies. You ate a piece of cheesecake last night? Now you have to work extra hard in the gym this morning. You ate "too many carbs" in one day? Oh, time to go on the longest run ever, past the point of feeling tired. I'm sure this all sounds very familiar to you. Don't feel guilty or shameful, because it all sounds *way* too familiar to me.

Unfortunately, so many of us have formed a negative and unhealthy relationship toward exercise. It really is such a shame... I believe exercise has the ability to have a positive and healthy effect on your heart, mind, and soul. It all begins with your perspective toward exercise and why you exercise. When looking at exercise, you can have a negative or positive outlook. First, let's start out by analyzing the negative perspective of exercise and the effects it can have on your body, mind, and image.

Negative Perspective

Having a negative perspective toward exercise is a lot more detrimental to your health, than you may think. A negative perspective has the potential to affect your overall physical health and even your mental health.

This perspective views exercise as a chore or a job. Viewing exercise as a chore causes you to dread the activity the whole time you're doing it. Remember when you were little and your mom made you clean up your room or do the dishes and you groaned at her request then always put the chore off until she came in your room yelling at you? Yeah, well many of us have that same attitude toward exercise. We think about exercising and we groan. This may be because we don't feel like being active or what we're considering "exercise" is running or lifting weights. Which, as I referred to earlier, doesn't always have to be the case. When we look at exercise, we look at all of the chores we hate to do (like when we were growing up) rather than all of the chores we *love* to do. So of course you're going to hate exercise! You're not choosing something you love! If you view exercise as a chore you hate, then you're going to hate it.

Having a negative perspective of physical activity can make exercise feel like a form of punishment. You're punishing yourself for overindulging the day before or maybe it's a pre-punishment for the food you're going to eat later that same day. The food you ate or are going to eat has left you feeling guilty and full of regret. You feel like the only way you can make up for it and get rid of this guilt, is by sweating it all off. You're punishing yourself with compensatory behavior for your actions. This is your way of erasing the bad food you ate.

This perspective also puts unrealistic demands on your body. You're forcing your body to do things you find no joy in. Why are you choosing to force your body to these measures? In an effort to feel skinny, pretty, or enough. You want to be accepted by society, your friends, and your family. Your friends are all going to the gym and getting the perfect summer body, so of course you have to do the same, but better. You feel the only way you can do that is by looking good. You want people to recognize you and your "perfect, hot" body. To hear the glorifying compliments, would make you feel so special and all the pain of physical exertion so worth it. You're looking to the world and the people in it for eternal joy and satisfaction.

How you feel about your image and how you want others to feel about your image lies at the core of how you feel about exercise. You either loathe your image or you're overly obsessed with your image. Both feelings toward your body can lead you to exercising out of desperate motives. You're exercising to either gain that perfect body image or to maintain that perfect body image. Whether you're exercising to gain or to maintain, you're leading your body down a road of rigid diets and exercise routines. You never allow yourself to break free from either because of the fear of potential outcomes- becoming fat, unloved, or unaccepted.

Maybe you feel tired, stressed, worried, or unhappy... maybe even all of those feelings. You're spending your life trying to keep up a perfect image and a perfect lifestyle. Ultimately, you're trapping yourself in a life full of overwhelming circumstances. Consequently, you're life is full of demands and lies. And ultimately, because you're filling your life with the lies of the world, you're missing out on the truth that Jesus declares over you. Not only that, but you're missing out on the great amount of love that Jesus has for you. Did you know that Jesus has an unexplainable, overwhelming, immeasurable kind of love for you? His love is something SO much more than the world can give you. So much more than "the perfect body image." Definitely so much more than you can give yourself. Nothing in this world will ever be able to outweigh the love, joy and peace that Jesus can give you. Unfortunately, it's all too easy to get caught up in the world's idea of love, to even realize the love that Jesus has for us. When we trap ourselves in restrictive lifestyles, we're missing out on the freeing life that God designed for us. He has so many plans for us to live healthy, happy lives. He even has plans for us to exercise and LOVE doing it!

Why We Need to Exercise

SO, I have a few questions for you to ponder: Why do we need to exercise? Why did God design exercise for us? What are his plans for exercise in our lives? Well, let me answer that simply with this- exercise is a way for us to glorify God with our bodies, treat our bodies with the best love and self-care they deserve, and appreciate our bodies for their strength.

Before anything else, exercise is a way for us to **glorify God and pursue His calling for our lives.** God gave each and every one of us a body to live in on this earth. As his children, we must take care of our bodies, so that we may fulfill our purpose on this earth. We all have the purpose of making disciples, as Jesus says in Matthew 28:19. We are also called to love God and love others, as said in Mark 12:30-31. This is the greatest commandment Jesus gave us, and can only be pursued if we have given our whole heart to Jesus. We cannot love His people if our needs supersede the importance of the needs of the people around us. As Christians, we must seek God before ourselves and our desires. In fact, we should not seek our desires at all, but rather God's desires. God does not desire for us to put exercise ahead of him and ahead of his people. To pursue God with your whole heart means to put Jesus over everything. This means even exercise and that perfect image you're thriving for.

Exercise should be a way for us to keep our bodies healthy and strong so that we may function for as long as Jesus planned for us to. By keeping our bodies healthy, we are adding to the longevity of our ministries. Investing in a healthy body, invests in the ministries of Jesus.

Exercise is also a form of discipline and responsibility. As Christians, we must discipline ourselves to incorporate healthy habits into our lives each day, so that we may be better overall. You and I must take responsibility into our hands to nourish and move our bodies, the way they were designed to. By taking these action steps, exercise turns into more than a selfish act. No longer is exercise beneficial only to you, but to the ministry of Jesus Christ too.

Once we can look at exercise and see it as a way for us to actively glorify God, we may then see it as **a form of self-love and self-care**. Because The Lord bought us with a HIGH price, we must honor our bodies. Our bodies are temples of the Holy Spirit, we must treat them as temples. We must love our bodies because the Lord carefully and uniquely designed every single one of our bodies. He designed you with every beautiful features, not flaws. The Lord created you with *no* flaws. The Lord loves you and cares for you, so why not love and care for yourself? Take care of the body the Lord has given you. Thank Him for this precious gift He has given you to live on this earth with. This body is not yours, but rather the Holy Spirit's. So how will you choose to honor God with it?

After you have answered that question for yourself, I hope you will take time to look at your body in a NEW way. Appreciate the body that the Lord has given you. And as you begin to exercise your body in this new, intentional way, may you also find appreciation in the strength your body has.

In addition to glorifying God and loving your body, exercise must also **give you a new appreciation for your body.** The Lord designed each of our bodies with the ability to be active in many different ways. Through exercise, we may realize this. Through exercise, we can realize how strong and how capable we truly are. You are not weak. You are not unworthy. You are **strong** and **worthy.** The world may scream differently, but the Lord tells you likewise. The Lord is telling you that you are capable of so many things in Him. Nothing is impossible through Him.

"For I can do everything through Christ who gives me strength." -Philippians 4:13

Overall- Coming at Exercise with a Positive Perspective

Once you understand why exercise is important and why God designed exercise, you will be able to develop a more positive view toward exercise. Exercise turns from a selfish ambition to a responsibility as a Christian on this earth. Slowly, those groans and grumbles towards exercise will disappear.

No longer will exercise be seen as a chore that *has* to be done. In fact, with the right attitude it will become an activity you build into your schedule, making time for it every day. Now, exercise is a chore you *love* to do. You are able to thrive in this chore because you have planted it in Jesus.

No longer is exercise seen as punishment for yesterday's food choices. Rather, you eat your food and move on. The guilt, shame, and regret is gone, because you have planted your beauty in Jesus. You don't find fulfillment in the food you eat and the exercise you performed to burn off those calories. You find fulfillment in Jesus. You find truth and joy and Jesus. Now, exercise is a part of your schedule on your good days and bad days. When you feel skinny and when you don't feel so skinny. You appreciate exercise because it is a way for you to love and take care of your body in the best way you know how.

With your new, God-designed perspective toward exercise, you don't have to force yourself to workout. In fact, you love to exercise now! You also don't demand a workout everyday. You realize, through Jesus, that you and your body need rest. Now, you are able to give your body rest, without fear and guilt filling your head. You appreciate your body for how strong it is and for everything it is capable of and everything God has designed it to be able to do, but you also realize it needs rest to be as strong as it is capable. Ultimately, your new perspective should be this, "This is the body I get to live in and thrive in on this earth. I have been given this body by God to love, steward, and treat with care."

Recipes...................Chapter 8

"Nikki's gunna bake bake bake."

Dad

Breakfast

(English) Muffin Monday:

Ingredients:
1 Food for Life 7 Grain English Muffin
1 egg
½ avocado
1 tomato slice
Salt and pepper to taste
1 tsp coconut oil/olive oil

Directions:
1. Melt ghee in a small pan on medium heat. Fry egg.
2. Toast english muffin (if desired) for 2 minutes.
3. Spread both sides of english muffin with avocado. Layer on egg and tomato slice. Sprinkle with salt and pepper.
4. Pack together. Enjoy at home or pack for the car ride to school!

Two Toasts Tuesday:

Ingredients:
2 slices of Food for Life 7 grain
¾ cup blueberries
½ cup Siggi's Vanilla Yogurt
Creamy peanut butter (Crazy
Richard's brand or Trader Joe's
Brand)
½ tsp cinnamon
1 tbsp chia seeds

Directions:
1. Toast both slices of 7 grain bread.
2. Spread toast with yogurt.
3. Warm blueberries on stovetop with a dash of water. Once they have reached a liquid-consistency, add the chia seeds. Pour onto the toast.
4. Drizzle peanut butter on top with a knife.
5. Enjoy!

Waffle Wednesday

Ingredients:
½ cup oat flour
¼ cup almond milk (I used Califia Farms Unsweetened Almond Milk)
1 egg
1 tbsp coconut oil, melted and cooled
1 tbsp pure maple syrup
1 tsp cinnamon
1 tsp pure vanilla extract
½ tsp baking powder

¼ tsp salt
Optional Toppings:
Blueberries, strawberries, and sliced bananas
Wild Friends Pumpkin Spice Peanut Butter
1 tsp chia seeds
Sprinkle of Cinnamon
1 tbsp Pure Maple Syrup (if desired, I'm not much of a maple syrup person)

Directions:
1. Turn on waffle-maker and allow it to warm up.
2. In a small bowl combine oat flour, baking powder, cinnamon, and salt.
3. In another small bowl whisk egg. Add almond milk, maple syrup, vanilla, and coconut oil. Mix well.
4. Pour wet ingredients into dry ingredients and mix well (be careful not to overmix).
5. Once the waffle maker has heated up, grease waffle maker. Pour in batter.
6. Once the green light has come on, remove waffles carefully.
7. Top with fruit. Sprinkle chia seeds. Sprinkle cinnamon.
8. Drizzle peanut butter and maple syrup.
9. Enjoy!

*These can be prepared ahead of time and frozen for a quick, on-the-go breakfast.
*If time and accessibility allows, saute blueberries for about 5 minutes on medium-low heat. This creates warm blueberries for a delicious waffle topping (:

Turmeric Oats Thursday

Ingredients:
½ cup oats
1 ½ cup water
1 tbsp chia seeds
1 tsp turmeric
1 tsp cinnamon
¼ tsp nutmeg
Sprinkle of black pepper
Almond milk (I used Califia Farms Unsweetened Almond Milk)
1 banana, mashed
Hemp seeds
Wild Friends Creamy Peanut Butter

Directions:
1. Boil water. Add oats and chia seeds. Lower to medium heat, cook for 5 minutes, or until excess water is gone and oats are thick and creamy. About halfway through, added mashed banana. Stir frequently.
2. Once oats are cooked, stir in spices. Splash almond milk if needed.
3. Pour oats into bowl. Sprinkle hemp seeds. Drizzle creamy peanut butter. (Top with any other desired toppings. Granola is a good topping for added crunch.)

French Toast Friday

Ingredients:
2 slices Food for Life cinnamon raisin
½ banana, half mashed
1 egg
3 tbsp unsweetened almond milk (I used Califia Farms)
1 tsp pure vanilla extract
½ tsp cinnamon
Toppings:
½ apple of choice, diced into cubes
Wild Friend's Pumpkin Spice Peanut Butter (or creamy PB)
1 tsp chia seeds
Sprinkle of cinnamon

Directions:
1. Preheat griddle or stove-top pan to medium high heat.
2. In a wide bowl mix together eggs, mashed banana half, milk, cinnamon, and vanilla.
3. Top with diced apple* Drizzle PB. Sprinkle chia seeds and cinnamon.

*If able to, in a small skillet saute diced apples with cinnamon for about 5 minutes on medium-low heat. I realize not everybody has this accessibility or time so this is completely optional, but does enhance flavor!

Smoothie Saturday (Green Smoothie)

Ingredients:
1 cup kale
1 cup spinach
½ frozen banana (chopped into slices)
Handful of frozen strawberries
Handful of frozen mango
⅓ avocado (creates thickness, adds healthy fats)
¾ cup almond milk (I used Califia Farms)
1 scoop vital proteins collagen peptides (or any protein you desire)
1 tbsp hemp seeds
1 tsp vanilla extract (for flavor)
Optional Toppings:
Purely Elizabeth granola
Justin's Dark Chocolate Peanut Butter Cup (THE best)
Peanut Buttah drizzle (always drizzle)
Cacao Nibs

Directions:
1. Blend kale, spinach, and a little bit of almond milk.
2. Blend in frozen fruits, avocado, hemp seeds, vital proteins, and vanilla extract. Adding in rest of almond milk as needed.
3. Pour into a glass jar. Admire the thick and creamy texture (for a lil bit because you know, usual).
4. Top with any of the above toppings, or whatever your heart desires! (those are just my all-time FAVORITES)

Sweet Potato Bowl Sunday

Ingredients:
1 sweet potato
Blueberries*
1 (5.3 oz) container of Siggi's
yogurt, any flavor (vanilla tastes
great with this bowl)
⅓ cup Purely Elizabeth granola
Creamy nut butter (I used Wild
Friends {Peanut Butter)
Chia seeds
Hemp seeds
Cinnamon

Directions:
1. Bake sweet potato: line baking sheet with aluminum foil. Stab sweet potato with fork a few times. Place on baking sheet and bake in oven for 45 minutes at 400°F. Flip to other side halfway through. Check occasionally.
2. Remove from oven. Slice in half. Place in bowl.
3. Pair it with yogurt and granola. Top with blueberries (however many your heart desires).
4. Sprinkle hemp seeds, chia seeds, and a generous amount of cinnamon (always). Drizzle peanut butter.
5. Enjoy!

*If time and accessibility allows, heat up blueberries in a small skillet for about 5 minutes on medium-low heat (can also heat them up in the microwave for about 45 seconds).

Classic Breakfast You Should Have Memorized

Basic Chia Seed Pudding

This is a yummy, fiber-filled breakfast that can all be prepared the night before and eaten the next day- at home, in the car, or your first period class! I love this recipe because it's packed with fiber, protein, and good fats so it will keep you full for HOURS.

Ingredients:
3 tbsp chia seeds
¾ cup almond milk (I used Califia Farms)
½ tsp pure vanilla extract
Sprinkle of salt
1 tbsp pure maple syrup (optional sweetener)
Toppings:
Creamy Peanut Butter (I used Wild Friends)
Desired fruit
Sprinkle of cinnamon
Hemp seeds
Granola (I used Purely Elizabeth)

Directions:
1. In a small container (a regular-sized mason jar works perfectly) combine all of the above ingredients.
2. Stir everything together, then shake. Allow it to sit for five minutes.
3. After five minutes the chia seeds will have clumped together. To spread chia seeds apart, either stir with

fork, breaking the clumps apart, or place mixture in blender and blend for about a minute.
4. Place in fridge overnight.
5. In the morning, the mixture will have thickened to a pudding-like mixture. This can be heated up in the microwave for about 1 minute or eaten cold!
6. Before eating, top with chosen fruit. Sprinkle cinnamon and hemp seeds. Drizzle peanut butter. Add about ⅓ cup of granola.
7. Enjoy in container on-the-go or in a bowl in your favorite comfy spot!

Basic Overnight Oats

This is a quick and easy recipe that can be prepared the night before to avoid any stress and lack of breakfast in the morning!

Ingredients:
½ cup oats
¾ cup almond milk (I used Califia Farms)
1 tbsp nonfat greek yogurt (I used Fage)
1 tbsp chia seeds
1 tbsp pure maple syrup (optional sweetener)
1 tsp cinnamon
1 tsp pure vanilla extract
Sprinkle of salt

Optional: 1 scoop of preferred protein powder and/or powder peanut butter
Toppings:
Desired fruit
Creamy peanut butter (I used Wild Friends*)

More greek yogurt
Granola (I used Purely Elizabeth)

Directions:
1. In a small container (or regular-sized mason jar) add oats, chia seeds, cinnamon, salt, (and protein powder/powder peanut butter). Stir to distribute ingredients.
2. Add almond milk, greek yogurt, vanilla extract, and maple syrup if you choose to add sweetener. Stir with spoon, then shake to really distribute all of the ingredients.
3. Place in fridge overnight.
4. In the morning, remove from fridge. You have two options now: heat it up on the stovetop/microwave OR eat cold.
5. Whichever way you choose, add your toppings (for an enhanced flavor) before devouring the whole bowl! Hehe (;

*you want to make sure you're using all-natural PB with minimal ingredients

Lunch

Easy "Snack Plate" Lunch

What You Need:
2 hard boiled eggs (or 3 all natural turkey slices)
½ cup baby carrots
2 stalks of celery, chopped
1 cup blueberries and/or strawberries
1 cup lesserevil avocado oil popcorn or 6 whole wheat crackers
2 tbsp Roots Original Hummus

Avocado Black Bean Sammie

Ingredients:
1 Food for Life 7 grain english muffin
Lantana Black Bean Hummus
⅓ Avocado
1 egg
Handful of spinach
Hemp seeds

Directions:
1. Fry egg in cast iron pan.
2. While egg is cooking, slice english muffin and toast.
3. Spread one side of english muffin with black bean hummus and other side with avocado. Sprinkle hemp seeds onto avocado (can also sprinkle salt and pepper for taste). Top egg onto sandwich. Pack handful of spinach in and close up that sandwich.

Egg Salad Sammie

Ingredients:
2 hard boiled eggs
1 tbsp Primal Kitchens Avocado Oil Mayo
1 celery stick, chopped
Salt & Pepper to taste
2 slices of whole grain/gluten free bread (I used Food for Life 7 grain)

Optional Sides:
1 cup carrots
1 tangerine*

Directions:
1. Mix hard-boiled eggs with mayo, chopped celery, and salt & pepper.
2. Spread on bread (I toasted mine).
3. Wrap up and take on the go with carrots and tangerine.

*Nix the candy for a sweet after snack and satisfy your sweet tooth with an all-natural snack (:

Grilled PB&J

Ingredients:
2 slices of Food for Life 7 grain bread
Wild Friends Creamy Peanut Butter
½ cup strawberries, diced
Ghee Butter
Chia seeds

Directions:
1. In a medium skillet, saute diced strawberries in ghee butter, stirring constantly.
2. Add chia seeds.
3. As strawberries soften, mash mixture, creating a jam-like substance.
4. Spread 1 slice of 7 grain with peanut butter. Spread the other slice with strawberry jam. Make a sandwich with slices.
5. Using the same skillet, heat sandwich in ghee butter, on medium-low heat.
6. Cook for about 1 minute. Flip. Cook for another minute.
7. Enjoy with some veggies and there's your easy peasy kiddie lunch(:

Kale Superfood Salad

Ingredients:
3 cups of kale
2 tbsp olive oil
¼ tsp Himalayan Sea Salt
¼ tsp Black Pepper
½ cup blueberries
¼ cup chopped strawberries
⅓ cup feta crumbles
¼ cup sunflower seeds

Directions:
1. Wash and dry kale. Place kale in medium to-go container. Evenly drizzle olive oil over kale. Massage kale with hands for about 1 minute, or until softened. Sprinkle sea salt and pepper.

2. Mix strawberries and blueberries into kale mixture.
3. Sprinkle feta crumbles and sunflower seeds on top.
4. Close container up and store in fridge for a quick and easy lunch the next day!

*add chicken (or any desired source of protein) for more protein

Pink Lady Spinach Salad

Ingredients:
2 cups spinach
1 chicken breast, baked and diced
½ pink lady apple
¼ cup pecans, chopped
2 tbsp goat cheese
2 tbsp raisins
For the dressing:
1 tbsp apple cider vinegar
1 tbsp olive oil

Directions:
1. Mix all of the ingredients together in a medium-sized bowl (to-go container).
2. For the dressing, mix vinegar and olive oil together. Drizzle over salad.

Quinoa Kale Salad

Ingredients:
2 cups kale
1 cup quinoa, cooked (following directions on package)
2 tbsp olive oil
¼ cup sliced almonds
⅓ cup goat cheese
Pepper to taste

Directions:
1. Place kale in medium sized bowl/to-go container. Drizzle olive oil over kale. Massage for about 1 minute, or until softened.
2. Add cooked quinoa to kale. Combine evenly. Sprinkle pepper.
3. Top with sliced almonds and goat cheese.

Waldorf Salad

Ingredients:
2 slices of Food for Life 7 Grain (or other whole grain bread, gluten free bread)
1 small can of tuna fish (or chicken), stored in water
⅛ cup Primal Kitchen's Avocado Oil Mayo
⅛ cup nonfat greek yogurt
¼ cup dried cranberries
¼ cup chopped walnuts
1 celery stick, chopped
Handful of spinach
Salt to taste
Pepper to taste

Directions:
1. Drain tuna.
2. In a small bowl combine tuna, greek yogurt, and mayo. Mix well.
3. Add chopped celery, cranberries, and chopped walnuts. Mix well. Sprinkle salt and pepper to taste.
4. Toast bread (if desired).
5. Add tuna and spinach to bread. Slice and enjoy! (or wrap up and save for a ggrab-and-go lunch the next day!)

Dinner

Classic Chicken Fajita Bowl

Ingredients:
Chicken Breast, stripped
1 Bell Pepper (red, yellow, or green), sliced
½ an onion, diced
½ avocado, diced
½ cup cooked wild rice (follow directions on package)
½ lime, sliced
Cilantro
Fajita spices (⅛ tsp cayenne powder, ½ tsp paprika, ½ tsp salt, ½ tsp pepper)
Olive oil

Directions:
1. Heat olive oil in a medium-sized pan (or wok) on medium heat. Add chicken strips to pan with about half of spice mixture. Cook until lightly browned, about 8 minutes. Set aside.
2. After, heat olive oil in a separate pan, on medium heat. Add peppers and onions and the rest of spices. Cook until softened, about 8 minutes.
3. In a small bowl place prepared rice, chicken, and veggies. Add diced avocado.
4. Sprinkle chopped cilantro and lime juice.
5. Enjoy!

Zucchini Shrimp Salad

Ingredients:
1 zucchini, spiralized
7 pieces of fresh shrimp
Sweet potato
Salt
Pepper
Chosen Foods Avocado Oil
Spray

Directions:
1. Preheat oven to 425 degrees fahrenheit.
2. Chop sweet potato into cubes. SPread on baking sheet. Spray with oil. Sprinkle salt and pepper. Bake for 30 minutes.
3. While sweet potatoes are cooking, warm shrimp on medium skillet.
4. Place spiralized zucchini in bowl. Top with shrimp and sweet potatoes.

Quinoa Casserole

Ingredients:
2 large chicken breasts, cooked and diced
2 cups quinoa, cooked
1 (15 oz) can organic black beans
1 (15 oz) can organic whole kernel corn
1 (24 oz) can diced tomatoes
1 packet all natural chili powder
1 cup mexican shredded cheese

Directions:
1. Preheat oven to 350.
2. Mix together quinoa, diced chicken, black beans, corn, diced tomatoes, and spices in a large bowl.
3. Pour mixture into an 8 x 11 pan. Coat with cheese.
4. Bake for 10 minutes, or until cheese is melted.
5. Remove from oven. Let cool for 5 minutes. Cut and serve.

Roasted Veggie Bowl

Ingredients:
½ sweet potato
Broccoli
Cauliflower
Chosen foods avocado oil spray
Salt
Pepper
Paprika
Chicken breast
Optional Toppings:
Avocado
Original hummus

Directions:
1. Preheat oven to 425.
2. Slice sweet potato into fries.
3. Line a baking sheet with aluminum foil. Lay out "fries," broccoli, and cauliflower on baking sheet. Also add chicken breast to pan. Spray avocado oil on chicken and veggies. Sprinkle salt, pepper, and paprika on chicken and veggies.

4. Place pan in oven and bake for 40 minutes at 425. Halfway through, flip veggies and check chicken.
5. Once ready, remove from oven. Place in bowl.
6. Add desired toppings.
7. Enjoy!

Sweet Potato Shepherd's Pie

_Ingredients:
3 medium-large sweet potatoes
1 pound of ground turkey, cooked
1 (15 oz) canned green beans
3 large carrots, chopped
1 cup vegetable broth
Almond milk
1 tbsp ghee butter
Pepper to taste
Paprika to taste

Directions:
1. Preheat oven to 400. Grease 8 x 11 pan.
2. Chop and slice sweet potatoes. Place in a medium saucepan and boil for about 8 minutes, or until softened.
3. In another medium saucepan boil carrots for about 10 minutes, or until softened.
4. Mix together carrots, green beans, ground turkey, vegetable broth, and spices in a medium bowl.
5. Mash and blend softened sweet potatoes, adding ghee butter and a splash of almond milk, to make creamy.
6. Pour into greased pan. Coat with sweet potatoes.
7. Bake for 25 minutes, or until sweet potatoes have browned.

Tuna Salad Bowl

Ingredients (for the tuna):
1 (5-6 oz) can of wild caught tuna
¼ cup Primal Kitchen avocado oil mayo
¼ cup chopped walnuts
⅛ cup dried cranberries (or raisins)
1 celery stick, chopped small
Salt
Pepper

Ingredients (for the sweet potato)
½ a sweet potato
3 cups water
1 cup cauliflower
3 cups water
Cinnamon
Salt
Pepper

Ingredients (for the kale):
2 cups of kale
1 tbsp olive oil
Salt
Pepper

Directions:
1. Chop sweet potato into small 1 inch cubes. Boil in water until softened (stick fork in middle to test, about 10-12 minutes).
2. On another burner, boil cauliflower in water until softened (about 5-7 minutes)
3. While sweet potatoes and cauliflower are boiling, prepare tuna. Drain water from tuna can. In a small bowl mix together drained tuna, mayo, walnuts,

cranberries, diced celery, and salt and pepper to taste. Set aside.
4. Next, place kale in a medium bowl. Drizzle olive oil over kale. Massage kale until softened. Sprinkle salt and pepper.
5. Drain sweet potatoes and cauliflower. Sprinkle salt, pepper, and cinnamon. Mix well.
6. Top kale with sweet potatoes, cauliflower, and tuna mixture.
7. Enjoy!

Vegetarian Stuffed Sweet Potato

Ingredients:
1 medium-sized sweet potato
½ (15 oz) can organic black beans
½ (15 oz) can organic whole kernel corn
1 roma tomato, diced
Cilantro, chopped
Black pepper
Chili Powder
Guacamole Ingredients:
1 avocado
2 tbsp salsa
Garlic salt
Black pepper
Juice of 1 lime slice

Directions:
1. Preheat oven to 425.
2. Wash sweet potato. Stab it with a fork all over. Bake in oven for 40 minutes.

3. Mash avocado. Stir in salsa, garlic salt, black pepper, and lime juice.
4. Slice ready sweet potato in half. Stuff with corn, black beans, and diced tomatoes. Sprinkle black pepper and chili powder.
5. Top with 3 big spoonfuls of guacamole. Garnish with cilantro.

Vegetarian Chili

Ingredients:
1 (15 oz) can Black beans, organic
1 (15 oz) can Kidney beans, organic
1 (15 oz) can Pinto beans, organic
1 (15 oz) can whole kernel corn, organic
1 (28 oz) can diced tomatoes
2 tbsp chili powder
1 ½ tsp cumin
1 tsp oregano
1 tsp garlic salt
¼ tsp cayenne pepper
1 tsp black pepper

Directions:
1. In a crockpot pour black beans, kidney beans pinto beans, corn, and tomatoes.
2. Measure out spices and sprinkle in mixture. Stir together, evenly distributing ingredients.
3. Set crock-pot to 30 minutes on high heat.

Snacks

Brown Rice Pudding With Raisins

Ingredients:
3 cups cooked brown rice
(follow cooking directions on
package)
3 cups unsweetened almond milk
(I used Califia Farms)
2 tbsp chia seeds
1 tbsp pure vanilla extract
⅓ cup raisins
½ tbsp ground cinnamon
¼ tsp nutmeg

Directions:
1. Combine brown rice, chia seeds, vanilla extract, and almond milk in a medium saucepan. Cook on medium heat for about 20 minutes, or until thick and creamy.
2. Stir in raisins, cinnamon, and nutmeg. Let cool.
3. Distribute into mason jars and store in refrigerator for an easy snack or on-the-go breakfast.

Chocolate Energy Balls

Ingredients:
1 cup pitted dates
2 tbsp almond butter
¼ cup almonds
1 scoop of cacao protein powder
1 tbsp cacao powder
1 tbsp hemp seeds
1 tbsp chia seeds
1 tbsp flax seeds
1 tsp vanilla extract
Sprinkle of salt
Almond milk (if needed to combine ingredients, I used Califia Farms)

Directions:
1. In a high-speed blender, blend dates and almonds, until broken down to tiny pieces.
2. Add vanilla extract, almond butter, protein powder, and cacao powder. Blend until combined.
3. Sprinkle in hemp seeds, chia seeds, flax seeds, and salt. Blend well. (Add almond extract if needed.)
4. Roll into small balls. Store in freezer.
5. Take on-the-go (do not need to be refrigerated).

Chocolate Oatmeal Protein Bars

Ingredients:
2 cup oats
1 cup peanut butter
¼ cup honey

½ cup coconut oil, melted
½ cup dried fruit (I used cranberries)
4 tbsp cacao powder
2 tbsp chia seeds
1 tsp pure vanilla extract
Sprinkle of salt

Directions:
1. In a medium bowl mix together peanut butter, vanilla extract, honey, and cooled coconut oil.
2. Add to wet ingredients- oats, dried fruit, chia seeds, cacao powder, and salt. Mix evenly.
3. Line 8 x 8 pan with parchment paper. Spread mixture in pan. Freeze for a few hours, until solid.
4. Once solid, cut into even squares. Move to container.
5. Take on-the-go as an easy snack!

Pecan Pie Bar

Ingredients:
2 cups pecans
2 cups dates
1 tsp pure vanilla extract
¼ tsp nutmeg
1 tsp cinnamon

Directions:
1. In a high-speed blender blend together dates and pecans.
2. Add vanilla extract. Sprinkle in nutmeg and cinnamon. Blend until ingredients are evenly broken down into tiny pieces.

3. Line a 8 x 8 pan with parchment paper. Spread mixture evenly in pan. Freeze for a few hours, or until solid.
4. Once solid, remove from freezer and cut into rectangles.
5. Store in freezer.
6. Take as an on-the-go snack.

Oatmeal Raisin Breakfast Cookies

Dry Ingredients:
1 cup Whole wheat flour
1 cup dry rolled oats
1 tsp baking soda
¼ tsp salt
1 tsp cinnamon
⅔ cup raisins
Wet Ingredients:
½ cup applesauce
1 egg
1 tsp vanilla extract
½ cup pure cane sugar (or coconut sugar)

Directions:
1. Preheat oven to 350F.
2. In a large bowl combine applesauce, sugar, and vanilla extract. Whisk in egg. Mix well.
3. In a medium bowl mix together whole wheat flour, dry rolled oats, baking soda, salt, and cinnamon. Mix until evenly distributed.

4. Add bowl of dry ingredients into large bowl of wet ingredients. Whisk together. Add in raisins. Mix well with a mixing spatula.
5. Scoop heaping teaspoons of batter onto cookie sheet, placing cookies about 1 inch apart.
6. Bake cookies at 350F for 8 minutes, or until lightly browned. Remove from oven and let cool for 5 minutes. Using a spatula, scrape cookies off pan sheet and set on wired rack.

Desserts

Chocolate Nice Cream

Ingredients:
2 bananas
2 tbsp cacao powder
Almond milk (if needed, I used Califia Farms)

Directions:
1. Cut banana into coins. Place banana coins on a cookie sheet (covered in parchment).
2. Freeze banana coins overnight (or at least 4 hours).
3. Once completely frozen, add banana coins to a high-speed blender. Blend until broken down (add almond milk if needed). Add cacao powder. Blend more.

Banana Bread

Wet Ingredients:
4 super ripe bananas mashed
⅛ cup greek yogurt
⅛ cup almond milk (I used Califia Farms)
2 eggs
¼ cup pure cane sugar (or coconut sugar)
2 tsp vanilla extract
Dry Ingredients:
2 cups whole wheat flour
1 tsp baking soda
1 tsp cinnamon (plus extra cinnamon for sprinkle)

1 tsp allspice
¼ tsp salt

Directions:
1. Preheat oven to 350 degrees fahrenheit. Grease bread pan.
2. Mash bananas in a medium-sized bowl. Whisk in eggs one at a time. Mix in greek yogurt, almond milk, cane sugar, and vanilla extract.
3. In a small bowl, whisk together flour, baking soda, cinnamon, allspice, and salt.
4. Combine dry ingredients with ingredients. Mix with a spatula until all ingredients are combined. Do not overstir.
5. Pour into greased bread pan. Sprinkle with cinnamon.
6. Place in oven. Bake for 40 minutes (or until toothpick comes out clean) covering with tin foil for last 10 minutes.

Maple Pecan Muffins

Ingredients:
For the muffins:
2 cups oat flour (oats processed)
2 tsp baking powder
2 eggs
½ cup almond milk (I used Califia Farms)
1 All Natural GoGo Squeez (or ⅓ cup applesauce, unsweetened)
¼ cup pure maple syrup
1 tsp pure vanilla extract
⅓ cup chopped pecans
For the glaze:

2 tbsp almond butter
2 tbsp almond milk (I used Califia Farms)
1 tbsp pure maple syrup
6 pecans chopped finely

Directions:
1. Preheat oven to 350.
2. In a medium-sized bowl whisk eggs. Whisk in applesauce pouch, milk, maple syrup, and vanilla extract.
3. In a small bowl combine oat flour, baking and baking powder. Mix into medium bowl of wet ingredients. Add chopped pecans.
4. Pour into 24 muffin cups. Bake for 13 minutes.
5. Remove from oven. Let cool for 5 minutes. Remove from pan and place on cooling rack.
6. Mix together almond butter, almond milk, and maple syrup. Once muffins have cooled, spread mixture over each muffin. Sprinkle chopped pecans on top.

Cinnamon Apple Muffins

Dry Ingredients:
1 ½ cups whole wheat flour
1 ⅓ tsp baking powder
½ tsp salt
1 ½ tsp cinnamon
¼ tsp nutmeg
Wet Ingredients:
4 Tbsp applesauce
½ cup almond milk (or other non-dairy milk, I used Califia Farms)

2 eggs
4 Tbsp pure maple syrup
1 tsp vanilla extract
1 ⅓ cups diced apple (I used granny smith)

Directions:

1. Preheat oven to 350F. Grease muffin pan with oil
2. In a large bowl mix together applesauce and maple syrup. Add in egg and vanilla. Mix well. Stir in milk.
3. In a medium bowl add whole wheat flour, baking powder, salt, cinnamon, and nutmeg. Whisk until ingredients are evenly distributed.
4. Add bowl of dry ingredients into bowl of wet ingredients. Mix well with spatula. Mix in diced apple, until evenly distributed. Do not over-mix.
5. Pour batter into greased muffin pan (about ¼ cup batter per muffin).
6. Bake muffins at 350F for 27 minutes, or until inserted toothpick (in the middle of muffin) comes out clean. When done, remove from oven and let sit for 10 minutes. Transfer to a wire rack and let muffins cool before storing. Muffins will last up to 3 days in room temperature, and about 6 days in when stored in refrigerator.

Pumpkin Bread

Dry Ingredients:
2 cups whole wheat flour
1 tsp baking powder
1 tbsp pumpkin pie spice

½ tbsp cinnamon
¼ tsp salt
Wet Ingredients:
1 cup pumpkin puree
¼ cup greek yogurt
2 eggs
1 tsp vanilla extract
½ cup coconut sugar (or coconut sugar)

Directions:
1. Preheat oven to 350 degrees fahrenheit. Grease bread pan.
2. Place pureed pumpkin in a medium-sized bowl. Whisk in eggs one at a time. Mix in greek yogurt, almond milk, sweetener, and vanilla extract.
3. In a small bowl, whisk together flour, baking powder, cinnamon, pumpkin pie spice, and salt.
4. Combine dry ingredients with ingredients. Mix with a spatula until all ingredients are combined. Do not overstir.
5. Pour into greased bread pan. Sprinkle with pumpkin pie spice.
6. Place in oven. Bake for 40 minutes (or until toothpick comes out clean) covering with tin foil for last 10 minutes.

Acknowledgements

Never did I think I would be writing a dedication for a book… my book nonetheless. So here's to all my supporters. First things first, Jesus. Thank you Jesus for being my number one supporter, my strength, my healer, and THE Greatest Love of all time. Sometimes I wonder what life without Jesus would look like, and the answer to that is nothing. Life without Jesus is nothing and life with Jesus is everything. Love. Joy. Grace. That is how I describe it.

Second, to my family. Thank you Dad for leading our family, for protecting, for providing, and for overcoming all the stress in the world, just so our family can be happy. Thank you for always showing interest in everything I do and making me feel like the most beautiful girl in the world. Most importantly, thank you for the countless amount of times you have rescued me (and my car) on the side of the road. I am still learning how to treat my car with the tender love and care it needs. Thank you Mamma for being the Godly woman that you are. Thank you for being there on my worst days. Thank you for pretty much being my best friend no matter what. I can't imagine what college will look like without me having the capability to come home and just cry in your arms. YOU, my dear, are the mom of the freaking year. And here's to my siblings… Kirstie, thank you for lifting me up and making me feel like I'm not alone (and taking me out to dinner more times than I can count). Courtney, thank you for voicing my thoughts. Thank you for giving me ENDLESS amounts of rides in high school; driving Tommy has allowed me to realize your pain. You're a life-saver. And Tommy, good ole Tommy, thank you for bringing the laughter to our family. Thank you for comforting me when I needed comfort. Thank you for choosing to follow Jesus. I'm so proud of you and I pray you continue to choose Jesus in these next few years of high school. Keep choosing the brighter side of life, kiddo.

Third, to my friends and leaders in my life. Thank you Lauren for being the best dang small group leader to ever walk this earth. You led me through my awkward middle school years all the way until now, all the way from silly friend problems to boy problems to encouraging me in my walk with God. Whenever I'm asked to think of a difference maker in my life, I think of you. You, Lauren, are a difference maker and a freaking game changer.

April, thank you for being there for me at Gauntlet, summer of 2016. Your words, your comfort and your love meant more than you will ever know. I am so dang blessed to have you as my cousin- partially, because I will get to say I have a cousin in the Olympics (don't let me down on this), but mostly because you have such a beautiful heart, for God and for His people. I love ya, Lirpa.

Thank you Emma Kate for being my sweet bestie throughout high school! SO thankful to have had you to walk alongside of through the troubles and hardships. Thank you for encouraging me and rooting for me even when I made the stupidest mistakes (cough cough Junior year UGH). Thank you for always hugging me when I drove to your house just to cry. Thank you for being there! I'm so ready to see God fulfill so many things in your life this next year!

Thank you Lil and Ciera for being my outside-of-school besties. You both met me in my middle school years and stuck around! Thank you for committing to our friendship even when at times I made it so hard for you to.

Lil, thank you for encouraging me to follow Jesus and being the best girlie to lead a Fuse group with!

Thank you Newspring Church. It is hard to put into words what I have seen in the last six years. Thank you for sharing the love of Jesus to the next generation in a way most churches cannot. Thank you for creating an atmosphere where teenagers can come and lay out everything, all their burdens and all their vulnerabilities. Thank you for providing us with tools to learn and grow in God. Through Fuse, God has given me the greatest community and showed me the greatest love and grace through that community. As I sit here writing this, I am trying to imagine what my life would be like without having a church like Newspring to attend, and it's not even imaginable. Newspring is my living proof of the church: how we are called to it and the impact that it has on God's people. So, thank you for the eternal impact you have had on my life and will have on many others.

Thank you my dear, sweet friend, Cole, for designing the incredible front cover and back cover for this book! You have such a God-given talent!

Thank you to the sweet girls who shared their stories with me. So many girls will read your stories and experience Jesus through them!

I also just want to acknowledge all of the companies I mentioned in the recipes: Food for life baking, Wild friends, Purely elizabeth, Vital proteins, Califia farms, Justin's, Siggi's, Perfect bar, Fage, Lesserevil, Lantana, Primal kitchen, Chosen food, and Gogo Squeeze! Such great coupons with quality products! These products are registered trademarks and inclusion in this book does not imply endorsement of its contents.

Notes

Chapter 2

1. *Eating Disorder Statistics.* ANAD. National Association of Anorexia Nervosa and Associated Disorders. 2017. Web. 24 Mar 2017.
2. *Anorexia Nervosa.* The Center for Eating Disorders. Sheppard Pratt Health System. 2015. Web. 30 Mar 2017.
3. *Amenorrhea.* Mayo Clinic. Mayo Foundation for Medical Education and Research (MFMER). 9 May 2014. Web. 29 Mar 2017.
4. *Bulimia Nervosa.* The Center for Eating Disorders. Sheppard Pratt Health System. 2015. Web. 24 Mar 2017.
5. *New in the DSM-5: Binge Eating Disorder.* NEDA. National Eating Disorders Association. 2016. Web. 24 Mar 2017.
6. Kratina, Karin. *Orthorexia Nervosa.* NEDA. National Eating Disorders ASsociation. 2016. Web. 24 Mar 2017.

Chapter 3

1. Pillar, Ryan. Personal Interview. 8 Dec 2016.
2. Hansen, Haley. *My Story- Better Late Than Never.* Hungry Haley. Squarespace. 8 July 2015. Web. 8 Dec. 2016.
3. Saravia, Lauren. Personal Interview. 25 Feb 2017.

Chapter 5

1. *All About the Fruit Group.* Choose My Plate. USDA. 26 Jul 2016. Web. 29 Mar. 2017.
2. *Tips to Help You Eat Fruits.* Choose My Plate. USDA. 7 Jan 2016. Web. 29 Mar 2017.
3. *All About the Vegetable Group.* Choose My Plate. USDA. 27 Jul 2016. Web. 29 Mar 2017.
4. *Tips to Help You Eat Vegetables.* Choose My Plate. USDA. 12 Jan. 2016. Web. 29 Mar 2017.
5. *All About the Grains Group.* Choose My Plate. USDA. 18 Oct 2016. Web. 27 Mar 2017.
6. *Tips to Help You Eat Grains.* Choose My Plate. USDA. 16 Jun 2015. Web. 29 Mar 2017.
7. *All About the Protein Foods Group.* Choose My Plate. USDA. 29 July 2016. Web. 29 Mar 2017.
8. *Tips for Making Wise Choices.* Choose My Plate. USDA. 21 Jan 2016. Web. 29 Mar 2017.
9. *All About the Dairy Group.* Choose My Plate. USDA. 29 Jul 2016. Web. 29 Mar 2017.
10. *Tips to Making Wise Choices.* Choose My Plate. USDA. 26 Jun 2015. Web. 29 Mar 2017.
11. Renee, Janet. *Will eating too few calories make you gain weight?* Livestrong. Leaf Group. 11 Jan 2016. Web. 29 Mar 2017.
12. *Eating Disorders and Hormones.* You and Your Hormones. Society for Endocrinology. 22 Dec 2016. Web. 29 Mar 2017.
13. Seidenfeld, M. E. K., & Rickert, V. I. *Impact of Anorexia, Bulimia and Obesity on the Gynecologic Health of Adolescents.* American Family Physician. American Academy of Family Physicians. 1 Aug 2001. Web. 29 Mar 2017.
14. *My Plate Checklist Calculator.* Choose My Plate. USDA. Jan 2016. Web. 29 Mar 2017.

15. Shotkoski, Melissa. Personal Interview. 3 Nov 2016.
16. Denny, Sharon. *Essential Nutrients for Women while Cutting Calories.* Eat Right. Academy of Nutrition and Dietetics. 30 Sep 2016. Web. 29 Mar 2017.
17. Cavazos, Miguel. *Carbs Before a Workout & Protein After.* Livestrong. Leaf Group. 18 Dec 2013. Web. 29 Mar 2017.
18. Shotkoski, Melissa. Personal Interview. 11 Nov 2016.
19. *Smart Snacking for Adults and Teens.* Eat Right. Academy of Nutrition and Dietetics. 2017. Web. 29 Mar 2017.

Chapter 6

1. *American Heart Association Recommendations for Physical Activity in Adults.* American Heart Association. 27 Jul 2016. Web. 29 Mar 2017.
2. Shotkoski, Melissa. Personal Interview. 14 Feb 2017.
3. *Endurance Exercise (Aerobic).* American Heart Association. 24 Mar 2015. Web. 29 Mar 2017.
4. *Examples of Physical Activities by Intensity.* U.S. Department of Health and Human Services. (1999). Promoting physical activity. Champaign, IL: Human Kinetics.
5. *Strength and Resistance Training Exercise.* American Heart Association. 24 Mar 2015. Web. 29 Mar 2017.
6. *Balance Exercise.* American Heart Association. 24 Mar 2015. Web. 29 Mar 2017.
7. *Flexibility Exercise (Stretching).* American Heart Association. 24 Mar 2015. Web. 29 Mar 2017.
8. *Physical activity improves quality of life.* American Heart Association. 2 Mar 2015. Web. 29 Mar 2017.
9. *Endorphins.* Good Therapy. 7 Aug. 2015. Web. 29 Mar 2017.

10. Robinson, L., Segal, J. & Smith, M. *The Mental Health Benefits of Exercise.* Help Guide. Jan 2017. Web. 29 Mar 2017.
11. White, Justin. *How Many Rest Days Do I Really Need?* Greatist. 29 Jun 2015. Web. 30 Mar 2017.
12. Bireline, Amanda. *The Importance of Recovery After Exercise.* NIFS. National Institute for Fitness and Sport. 5 May 2015. Web. 29 Mar 2017.
13. Cavazos, Miguel. *Carbs Before a Workout & Protein After.* Livestrong. Leaf Group. 18 Dec 2013. Web. 29 Mar 2017.
14. Cunningham, Eleese. *How to Fuel Your Workout.* Eat Right. Academy of Nutrition and Dietetics. 20 Jun 2016. Web. 29 Mar 2017.

Get Connected with Nicole!

Blog: fearfullyandwonderfullybalanced.wordpress.com
Instagram Handle: wonderfullybalanced
Email: wonderfullybalanced@gmail.com
Phone Number: 864-991-6867

Made in the USA
Middletown, DE
26 April 2017